COOKSHELF
Baking

Emma Patmore

This is a Parragon Book
This edition published in 2000
Parragon
Queen Street House
4 Queen Street
Bath BA1 1HE,UK

Hardback ISBN: 0-75254-132-3
Paperback ISBN:0-75254-138-2

Printed in China

Note
Cup measurements in this book are for American cups. Tablespoons are
assumed to be 15 ml. Unless otherwise stated, milk is assumed to be full fat,
eggs are medium and pepper is freshly ground black pepper.

Contents

Introduction   4

Family Favourites   6

Breads & Savouries   62

Vegetarian Baking   138

Cakes   160

Biscuits (Cookies)   210

Index   256

Introduction

This beautifully illustrated book brings you all the skills you need to recreate some of the best-loved traditional baking dishes. It also shows you how to experiment with some of the exciting contemporary ingredients now readily available in leading supermarkets.

Perfectly clear step-by-step instructions guide you through the techniques needed to mastermind all those baking favourites that have been savoured and enjoyed from generation to generation.

FAMILY FAVOURITES

Experience the sweet pleasure of a wonderful selection of everyday and special occasion desserts in Chapter 1 as it shows you how to make rich, gooey and irresistible puddings such as Pavlova, Fruit Crumble, Queen of Puddings and tasty sticky chocolate puddings. Everyone's favourite is sure to be included.

This chapter also helps you to perfect your pastry so that you are guaranteed success with such timeless cookery classics as Treacle Tart, Apple Tart Tatin, Apricot & Cranberry Frangipane and Egg Custard Tart.

BREADS & SAVOURIES

Making bread at home is great fun and allows you to experiment with all sorts of ingredients, such as sun-dried tomatoes, garlic, mangoes and olive oil, to create versatile and delicious variations of modern breads. Chapter 2 also shows you how to spice-up all sorts of savouries with exciting adaptations of traditional flans, pies and scones, such as Cheese & Mustard Scones and delicious Onion Tart.

VEGETARIAN COOKING

Vegetarian recipes full of delicious wholesome ingredients, which are every bit as good as traditional baking favourites, have been created in Chapter 3. Recipes include Lentil & Red (Bell) Pepper Flan, Date & Apricot Tart, Pineapple Upside-down Cake and Brazil Nut & Mushroom Pie.

CAKES & BISCUITS

Transform traditional cakes and biscuits into a real tea-time extravaganza with some new adaptations of old tea-time favourites in Chapters 4 and 5.

Irresistible cake recipes, such as Marbled Chocolate Cake, Olive Oil Fruit & Nut Cake, Gingerbread and Meringues, are included as are delicious biscuit (cookie) recipes, such as Chocolate Chip Cookies and Ginger Biscuits (Cookies). These recipes are quick and easy to make and are sure to be winners with all of the family.

MAKING CAKES

With all baking recipes, there are some basic principles that apply and this is especially true of cake making:

- Start by reading the recipe all the way through.
- Weigh all the ingredients accurately and do basic preparation, such as grating and chopping, before you start cooking.
- Basic cake-making ingredients should be kept at room temperature.
- Mixtures that are creamed together, a process which involves creaming butter and sugar together, should be almost white and have a 'soft dropping' consistency. This can be done by hand, but using a hand-held electric mixer will save you time and effort.
- 'Folding in' is achieved by using a metal spoon or spatula and working as gently as possible to fold through the flour or dry ingredients in a figure of eight movement.
- Do not remove a cake from the oven until it is fully cooked. To test if a cake is cooked, press the surface lightly with your fingertips – it should feel springy to the touch. Alternatively, insert a fine metal skewer into the centre of the cake – it will come out clean if the cake is cooked through.
- Leave cakes in their tins (pans) to cool before carefully turning out on to a wire rack to cool completely.

MAKING PIES & TARTS

When making the pies or tarts in the book, follow these basic principles:

- Sieve (strain) the dry ingredients into a large mixing bowl, add the diced fat and toss it through the flour
- Gently rub the fat between your fingertips a little at a time until the mixture looks like fine breadcrumbs and, as you rub in the mixture, lift your hands up to aerate the mixture as it falls back into the bowl.
- Bind the mixture with iced water or other liquid, using just enough to make a soft dough. Wrap the dough and leave to chill for at least 30 minutes.

Family Favourites

No true meal is really complete without a pudding and this chapter indulges the reader with a hearty and wholesome collection of some of the best-loved family favourites. Fruit puddings, chocolate puddings, lemon puddings and crumbly puddings – they are all fun, easy to make and deliciously delightful to eat. This chapter also offers some new surprises for old-fashioned puddings, leaving you with the difficult decision of which to try first; will it be Plum Cobbler or Mini Frangipane Tartlets with Lime?

Soft, crumbly and melt-in-the-mouth, pastry holds the secret to success with a wide variety of magnificent dishes. Shortcrust pastry (pie dough) is used in several recipes in this chapter and it is important to remember that a light touch when preparing the pastry will give a much better result.

Where 'fresh ready-made shortcrust pastry (pie dough)' and 'fresh ready-made puff pastry (pie dough)' is specified in the recipes, the quality that you get from the supermarket products is extremely good and saves you time on certain recipes.

Eve's Pudding

Serves 6

INGREDIENTS

450 g/1 lb cooking apples,
  peeled, cored and sliced
75 g/2³/4 oz/¹/3 cup
  granulated sugar
1 tbsp lemon juice
50 g/1³/4 oz/¹/3 cup sultanas
  (golden raisins)

75 g/2³/4 oz/¹/3 cup butter
75 g/2³/4 oz/¹/3 cup caster
  (superfine) sugar
1 egg, beaten
150 g/5¹/2 oz/1¹/4 cups self-
  raising flour
3 tbsp milk

25 g/1 oz/¹/4 cup flaked
  (slivered) almonds
custard or double (heavy)
  cream, to serve

1 Grease an 850 ml/
  1½ pint/3½ cup
ovenproof dish.

2 Mix the apples with
  the sugar, lemon juice
and sultanas (golden
raisins). Spoon the mixture
into the greased dish.

3 Cream the butter and
  caster (superfine)
sugar together until pale.
Gradually add the egg.

4 Carefully fold in the
  self-raising flour and
stir in the milk to give a
soft, dropping consistency.

5 Spread the mixture
  over the apples and
sprinkle with the flaked
(slivered) almonds.

6 Bake in a preheated
  oven, 180°C/350°F/Gas
Mark 4, for 40-45 minutes
until the sponge is golden
brown.

7 Serve the pudding hot,
  with custard or double
(heavy) cream.

COOK'S TIP

*To increase the almond
flavour of this pudding, add
25 g/1 oz/¹/4 cup ground
almonds with the flour
in step 4.*

Queen of Puddings

Serves 8

INGREDIENTS

600 ml/1 pint/2 1/2 cups milk
25 g/1 oz/6 tsp butter
225 g/ 8 oz/1 1/4 cups caster
(superfine) sugar

finely grated rind of 1 orange
4 eggs, separated
75 g/2 3/4 oz/3/4 cup fresh
breadcrumbs

pinch of salt
6 tbsp orange marmalade

1 Grease a 1.5 litre/ 2 3/4 pint/6 cup ovenproof dish.

2 To make the custard, heat the milk in a pan with the butter, 50 g/ 1 3/4 oz/1/4 cup of the caster (superfine) sugar and the grated orange rind until just warm.

3 Whisk the egg yolks in a bowl. Gradually pour the warm milk over the eggs, stirring.

4 Stir the breadcrumbs into the pan, then transfer the mixture to the prepared dish and leave to stand for 15 minutes.

5 Bake in a preheated oven, 180°C/350°F/Gas Mark 4, for 20-25 minutes until the custard has just set. Remove the custard from the oven but do not turn the oven off.

6 To make the meringue, whisk the egg whites with a pinch of salt until they stand in soft peaks. Whisk in the remaining sugar, a little at a time.

7 Spread the orange marmalade over the cooked custard. Top with the meringue, spreading it right to the edges of the dish.

8 Return the pudding to the oven and bake for a further 20 minutes until the meringue is crisp and golden.

Bread & Butter Pudding

Serves 6

INGREDIENTS

200 g/7 oz white bread, sliced
50 g/1³/₄ oz/10 tsp butter,
softened
25 g/1 oz/2 tbsp sultanas
(golden raisins)

25 g/1 oz mixed (candied) peel
600 ml/1 pint/2¹/₂ cups milk
4 egg yolks
75 g /2³/₄ oz/¹/₃ cup caster
(superfine) sugar

¹/₂ tsp ground mixed spice
(allspice)

1 Grease a 1.2 litre/ 2 pint/5¹/₃ cup ovenproof dish.

2 Remove the crusts from the bread (optional) and spread with butter. Cut into quarters.

3 Arrange half of the buttered bread slices in the prepared ovenproof dish. Sprinkle half of the sultanas (golden raisins) and mixed (candied) peel over the top of the bread.

4 Place the remaining bread slices over the fruit, and then sprinkle over the reserved fruit.

5 To make the custard, bring the milk almost to the boil. Whisk together the egg yolks and the sugar in a bowl, then pour in the warm milk.

6 Strain the warm custard through a sieve. Pour the custard over the bread slices.

7 Leave to stand for 30 minutes, then sprinkle with the ground mixed spice (allspice).

8 Place the ovenproof dish in a roasting tin (pan) half-filled with hot water.

9 Bake in a preheated oven, 200°C/400°F/ Gas Mark 6, for 40-45 minutes until the pudding has just set. Serve warm.

Plum Cobbler

Serves 6

INGREDIENTS

1 kg/2^1/4 lb plums, stones
    removed and sliced
100 g/3^1/2 oz /^{1}/3 cup caster
    (superfine) sugar
1 tbsp lemon juice

250 g/9 oz/2^1/4 cups plain (all-
    purpose) flour
75 g/2^3/4 oz/^{1}/3 cup
    granulated sugar
2 tsp baking powder
1 egg, beaten

150 ml/^{1}/4 pint/^{2}/3 cup
    buttermilk
75 g/2^3/4 oz/^{1}/3 cup butter,
    melted and cooled
double (heavy) cream, to serve

1 Lightly grease a
    2 litre/3½ pint/8 cup
ovenproof dish.

2 Mix together the
    plums, caster
(superfine) sugar, lemon
juice and 25 g/1 oz/¼ cup
of the plain (all-purpose)
flour.

3 Spoon the mixture
    into the prepared dish.

4 Combine the
    remaining flour,
granulated sugar and
baking powder in a bowl.

5 Add the beaten egg,
    buttermilk and cooled
melted butter. Mix gently
to form a soft dough.

6 Place spoonfuls of the
    dough on top of the
fruit mixture until it is
almost covered.

7 Bake in a preheated
    oven, 190°C/375°F/Gas
Mark 5, for 35-40 minutes
until golden brown.

8 Serve the pudding
    piping hot, with
double (heavy) cream.

COOK'S TIP

*If you cannot find
buttermilk, try using
soured cream.*

Blackberry Pudding

Serves 4

INGREDIENTS
---

450 g/1 lb blackberries
75 g/2³/4 oz/¹/3 cup caster
    (superfine) sugar
1 egg

75 g/2³/4 oz/¹/3 cup soft
    brown sugar
75 g/2³/4 oz/¹/3 cup butter,
    melted

8 tbsp milk
125 g/4 ½ oz self-raising flour

---

1 Grease an 850 ml/
1 ½ pint/3 ½ cup
ovenproof dish.

2 In a large bowl, gently
mix the blackberries
and caster (superfine) sugar
until well combined.

3 Transfer the blackberry
mixture to the
prepared ovenproof dish.

4 Beat the egg and soft
brown sugar in a
separate bowl. Stir in the
melted butter and milk.

5 Sieve (strain) the flour
into the egg and butter

mixture and fold together
lightly to form a smooth
batter.

6 Carefully spread the
batter over the
blackberry and sugar
mixture in the ovenproof
dish, covering the fruit.

7 Bake the pudding in
a preheated oven,
180°C/350°F/Gas Mark
4, for about 25-30 minutes
until the topping is firm
and golden.

8 Sprinkle the pudding
with a little sugar and
serve hot.

VARIATION

*You can add 2 tablespoons
of cocoa powder to the batter
in step 5, if you prefer a
chocolate flavour.*

Raspberry Shortcake

Serves 8

INGREDIENTS

175 g/6 oz/1¹/2 cups self-
raising flour
100 g/3¹/2 oz/¹/3 cup butter,
cut into cubes
75 g/2³/4 oz/¹/3 cup caster
(superfine) sugar

1 egg yolk
1 tbsp rose water
600 ml/1 pint/2¹/2 cups
whipping cream, whipped
lightly

225 g/8 oz raspberries, plus a
few for decoration

TO DECORATE:
icing (confectioners') sugar
mint leaves

1 Lightly grease 2 baking trays (cookie sheets).

2 To make the shortcakes, sieve (strain) the flour into a bowl.

3 Rub the butter into the flour with your fingers until the mixture resembles breadcrumbs.

4 Stir the sugar, egg yolk and rose water into the mixture and bring together to form a soft dough. Divide the dough in half.

5 Roll each piece of dough to a 20 cm/ 8 inch round and lift each one on to a prepared baking tray (cookie sheet). Crimp the edges of the dough.

6 Bake in a preheated oven, 190°C/375°F/Gas Mark 5, for 15 minutes until lightly golden. Transfer the shortcakes to a wire rack and leave to cool.

7 Mix the cream with the raspberries and spoon on top of one of the shortcakes. Top with the

other shortcake round, dust with a little icing (confectioners') sugar and decorate with the extra raspberries and mint leaves.

COOK'S TIP

The shortcake can be made a few days in advance and stored in an airtight container until required.

Pavlova

Serves 6

INGREDIENTS

3 egg whites
pinch of salt
175 g/6 oz/³/4 cup caster
(superfine) sugar

300 ml/¹/2 pint/1¹/4 cups
double (heavy) cream,
lightly whipped

fresh fruit of your choice
(raspberries, strawberries,
peaches, passion fruit, cape
gooseberries)

1 Line a baking sheet (cookie sheet) with a sheet of baking parchment.

2 Whisk the egg whites with the salt in a large bowl until soft peaks form.

3 Whisk in the sugar a little at a time, whisking well after each addition until all of the sugar has been incorporated.

4 Spoon three-quarters of the meringue on to the baking sheet (cookie sheet), forming a round 20 cm/8 inches in diameter.

5 Place spoonfuls of the remaining meringue all around the edge of the round so they join up to make a nest shape.

6 Bake in a preheated oven, 140°C/275°F/Gas Mark 1, for 1¼ hours.

7 Turn the heat off, but leave the pavlova in the oven until completely cold.

8 To serve, place the pavlova on a serving dish. Spread with the lightly whipped cream, then arrange the fresh fruit on top.

COOK'S TIP

It is a good idea to make the pavlova in the evening and leave it in the turned-off oven overnight.

Sticky Chocolate Pudding

Serves 6

INGREDIENTS

125 g/4¹/₂ oz/¹/₂ cup butter, softened
150 g/5¹/₂ oz/³/₄ cup soft brown sugar
3 eggs, beaten
pinch of salt
25 g/1 oz cocoa powder

125 g/4¹/₂ oz/1 cup self-raising flour
25 g/1 oz dark chocolate, chopped finely
75 g/2³/₄ oz white chocolate, chopped finely

SAUCE:
150 ml/5 fl oz/²/₃ cup double (heavy) cream
75 g/2³/₄ oz/¹/₃ cup soft brown sugar
25 g/1 oz/6 tsp butter

1 Lightly grease 6 individual 175 ml/6 fl oz/³/₄ cup pudding basins (molds).

2 Cream together the butter and sugar until pale and fluffy. Beat in the eggs a little at a time.

3 Sieve (strain) the salt, cocoa powder and flour into the creamed mixture and fold through the mixture. Stir the chopped chocolate evenly into the mixture.

4 Divide the mixture between the prepared pudding basins (molds). Lightly grease 6 squares of foil and use them to cover the basins (molds). Press around the edges to seal.

5 Place the basins (molds) in a roasting tin (pan) and add boiling water to come halfway up the sides of the basins (molds).

6 Bake in a preheated oven, 180°/350°F/Gas Mark 4, for 50 minutes, or until a skewer inserted into the centre comes out clean. Remove the basins (molds) from the tin and set aside.

7 To make the sauce, put the cream, sugar and butter into a pan and bring to the boil over a gentle heat. Simmer gently until the sugar has dissolved.

8 Turn the puddings out on to serving plates, pour the sauce over the top and serve immediately.

Chocolate Brownie Roulade

Serves 8

INGREDIENTS

150 g/5^1/2 oz dark chocolate, broken into pieces
3 tbsp water
175 g/6 oz/^{3}/4 cup caster (superfine) sugar

5 eggs, separated
25 g/1 oz/2 tbsp raisins, chopped
25 g/1 oz pecan nuts, chopped
pinch of salt

300 ml/^{1}/2 pint/1^1/4 cups double (heavy) cream, whipped lightly
icing (confectioners') sugar, for dusting

1 Grease a 30 × 20 cm/ 12 × 8 inch swiss roll tin (pan) and line with greased baking parchment.

2 Melt the chocolate with the water in a small saucepan over a low heat until the chocolate has just melted. Leave to cool.

3 Whisk the sugar and egg yolks for 2-3 minutes until thick. Fold in the cooled chocolate, raisins and pecan nuts.

4 Whisk the egg whites with the salt. Fold a

quarter of the egg whites into the chocolate mixture, then lightly fold in the rest.

5 Transfer the mixture to the prepared tin (pan) and bake in a preheated oven, 180°C/350°F/ Gas Mark 4, for 25 minutes until risen and just firm to the touch. Leave to cool before covering with a sheet of non-stick baking parchment and a damp clean tea towel (dish cloth). Leave to cool completely.

6 Turn the roulade out on to another piece of

baking parchment dusted with icing (confectioners') sugar and remove the lining paper.

7 Spread the cream over the roulade. Starting from a short end, roll the sponge away from you using the paper to guide you. Trim the ends of the roulade to make a neat finish and transfer to a serving plate. Leave to chill in the refrigerator until ready to serve. Dust with a little icing (confectioners') sugar before serving, if wished.

One Roll Fruit Pie

Serves 8

INGREDIENTS

PASTRY (PIE DOUGH):
175 g/6 oz/1¹/₂ cups plain
(all-purpose) flour
100 g/3¹/₂ oz/¹/₃ cup butter,
cut into small pieces
1 tbsp water
1 egg, separated

sugar cubes, crushed, for
sprinkling

FILLING:
600 g/1¹/₂ lb prepared fruit
(rhubarb, gooseberries,
plums, damsons)

75 g/3 oz/6 tbsp soft brown
sugar
1 tbsp ground ginger

1 Grease a large baking tray (cookie sheet).

2 To make the pastry (pie dough), place the flour and butter in a mixing bowl and rub in the butter with your fingers. Add the water and work the mixture together until a soft pastry (pie dough) has formed. Wrap and leave to chill in the refrigerator for 30 minutes.

3 Roll out the chilled pastry (pie dough) to a round about 35 cm/14 inches in diameter.

4 Transfer the round to the centre of the greased baking sheet (cookie sheet). Brush the pastry (pie dough) with the egg yolk.

5 To make the filling, mix the prepared fruit with the brown sugar and ginger and pile it into the centre of the pastry.

6 Turn in the edges of the pastry (pie dough) all the way around. Brush the surface of the pastry (pie dough) with the egg white and sprinkle evenly with the crushed sugar cubes.

7 Bake in a preheated oven, 200°C/400°F/Gas, Mark 6 for 35 minutes, or until golden brown. Serve warm.

Fruit Crumble Tart

Serves 8

INGREDIENTS

PASTRY (PIE DOUGH):
150 g/5 oz/1^{1}/4 cups plain (all-purpose) flour
25 g/1 oz/5 tsp caster (superfine) sugar
125 g/4^{1}/2 oz/^{1}/2 cup butter, cut into small pieces
1 tbsp water

FILLING:
250 g/9 oz raspberries
450 g/1 lb plums, halved, stoned and chopped roughly
3 tbsp demerara (brown crystal) sugar

TO SERVE:
single (light) cream

TOPPING:
125 g/4^{1}/2 oz/1 cup plain (all-purpose) flour
75 g/2^{3}/4 oz/^{1}/3 cup demerara (brown crystal) sugar
100 g/3^{1}/2 oz/^{1}/3 cup butter, cut into small pieces
100 g/3^{1}/2 oz chopped mixed nuts
1 tsp ground cinnamon

1 To make the pastry (pie dough), place the flour, sugar and butter in a bowl and rub in the butter with your fingers. Add the water and work the mixture together until a soft pastry (pie dough) has formed. Wrap and leave to chill for 30 minutes.

2 Roll out the pastry (pie dough) to line the base of a 24 cm/9^{1}/2 inch loose-bottomed quiche/flan tin (pan). Prick the base of the pastry (pie dough) with a fork and leave to chill for about 30 minutes.

3 To make the filling, toss the raspberries and plums together with the sugar and spoon into the pastry case (pie shell).

4 To make the crumble topping, combine the flour, sugar and butter. Work the butter into the flour with your fingers until the mixture resembles coarse breadcrumbs. Stir in the nuts and cinnamon.

5 Sprinkle the topping over the fruit and bake in a preheated oven, 200°C/400°F/Gas Mark 6, for 20-25 minutes until golden. Serve the tart with single (light) cream.

Cheese & Apple Tart

Serves 8

INGREDIENTS

175 g/6 oz/1½ cups self-
   raising flour
1 tsp baking powder
pinch of salt
75 g/2¾ oz/⅓ cup soft
   brown sugar

100 g/3½ oz stoned dates,
   chopped
500 g/1lb 2 oz dessert apples,
   cored and chopped
50 g /1¾ oz/¼ cup walnuts,
   chopped

50 ml/2 fl oz/¼ cup
   sunflower oil
2 eggs
175 g/6 oz Red Leicester
   cheese, grated

1 Grease a 23 cm/9½ inch loose-bottomed quiche/flan tin (pan) and line with baking parchment.

2 Sieve (strain) the flour, baking powder and salt into a bowl. Stir in the brown sugar and the chopped dates, apples and walnuts. Mix together until well combined.

3 Beat the oil and eggs together and add the mixture to the dry ingredients. Stir until well combined.

4 Spoon half of the mixture into the tin (pan) and level the surface.

5 Sprinkle with the cheese, then spoon over the remaining cake mix, spreading it to the edges of the tin (pan).

6 Bake in a preheated oven, 180°C/350°F/Gas Mark 4, for 45-50 minutes or until golden and firm to the touch.

7 Leave to cool slightly in the tin. Serve warm.

COOK'S TIP

This is a deliciously moist tart. Any leftovers should be stored in the refrigerator and heated to serve.

Apple Tart Tatin

Serves 8

INGREDIENTS

125 g/4^1/2 oz/^{1}/2 cup butter
125 g/4^1/2 oz/^{1}/2 cup caster
(superfine) sugar
4 dessert apples, cored and
quartered

250 g/9 oz fresh ready-made
shortcrust pastry (pie
dough)

crème fraîche, to serve

1 Heat the butter and
sugar in a 23 cm/9 inch
ovenproof frying pan
(skillet) over a medium
heat for 5 minutes until the
mixture begins to
caramelize. Remove from
the heat.

2 Arrange the apple
quarters, skin side
down, in the pan, taking
care as the butter and sugar
are very hot. Return the
pan (skillet) to the heat and
simmer for 2 minutes.

3 On a lightly floured
surface, roll out the

pastry (pie dough) to form
a circle just a little larger
than the pan.

4 Place the pastry (pie
dough) over the apples,
press down and tuck in the
edges to seal the apples
under the layer of pastry.

5 Bake in a preheated
oven, 200°C/400°F/Gas
Mark 6, for 20-25 minutes
until golden. Remove from
the oven and leave to cool
for about 10 minutes.

6 Place a serving plate
over the frying pan

(skillet) and invert so
that the pastry forms the
base of the turned-out
tart. Serve warm with
crème fraîche.

VARIATION

*Replace the apples with
pears, if you prefer. Leave
the skin on the pears, cut
them into quarters and then
remove the core.*

Treacle Tart

Serves 8

INGREDIENTS

250 g/ 9 oz fresh ready-made
    shortcrust pastry
350 g/12 oz/1 cup golden
    (light corn) syrup
125 g/4^1/$_2$ oz/2 cups fresh
    white breadcrumbs

125 ml/4 fl oz/^{1}/$_2$ cup double
    (heavy) cream
finely grated rind of ^{1}/$_2$ lemon
    or orange

2 tbsp lemon or orange juice
custard, to serve

1 Roll out the pastry (pie dough) to line a 20 cm/8 inch loose-bottomed quiche/flan tin (pan), reserving the pastry (pie dough) trimmings. Prick the base of the pastry (pie dough) with a fork and leave to chill in the refrigerator.

2 Using a shaped pastry cutter or a sharp knife, cut out small shapes from the reserved pastry (pie dough) trimmings, such as leaves, stars or hearts, to decorate the top of the tart.

3 In a bowl, mix together the golden (light corn) syrup, breadcrumbs, cream and grated lemon or orange rind and lemon or orange juice.

4 Pour the mixture into the pastry case (pie shell) and decorate the edges of the tart with the pastry (pie dough) cut-outs.

5 Bake in a preheated oven, 190°C/375°F/Gas Mark 5, for 35-40 minutes or until the filling is just set.

6 Leave the tart to cool slightly in the tin. Turn out and serve with custard.

VARIATION

Use the pastry (pie dough) trimmings to create a lattice pattern on top of the tart, if preferred.

Apple & Mincemeat Tart

Serves 8

INGREDIENTS

PASTRY (PIE DOUGH):
150 g/5 oz/1^1/4 cups plain (all-purpose) flour
25 g/1 oz/5 tsp caster (superfine) sugar

125 g/4^1/2 oz/^{1}/2 cup butter, cut into small pieces
1 tbsp water

FILLING:
411 g/14^1/2 oz jar mincemeat

3 dessert apples, cored
1 tbsp lemon juice
40 g/1^1/2 oz/6 tsp golden (light corn) syrup
40 g/1^1/2 oz/9 tsp butter

1 To make the pastry (pie dough), place the flour and caster (superfine) sugar in a large mixing bowl and rub in the butter with your fingertips.

2 Add the water and work the mixture together until a soft pastry (pie dough) has formed. Wrap and leave to chill in the refrigerator for 30 minutes.

3 On a lightly floured surface, roll out the dough and line a 24 cm/ 9½ inch loose-bottomed quiche/flan tin (pan). Prick the dough with a fork and leave to chill for 30 minutes.

4 Line the pastry case (pie shell) with foil and baking beans. Bake the case (shell) in a preheated oven, 190°C/375°F/ Gas Mark 5, for 15 minutes. Remove the foil and beans and cook for 15 minutes.

5 Grate the apples and mix with the lemon juice and mincemeat.

Spoon into the baked pastry case (pie shell).

6 Melt the syrup and butter together and pour it over the mincemeat mixture.

7 Return the tart to the oven and bake for about 20 minutes or until firm. Serve warm.

VARIATION

Add 2 tbsp sherry to spice up the mincemeat, if you wish.

Custard Tart

Serves 8

INGREDIENTS

PASTRY (PIE DOUGH):
150 g/5^1/$_2$ oz plain
(all-purpose) flour
25 g/1 oz/5 tsp caster
(superfine) sugar
125 g/4^1/$_2$ oz/^{1}/$_2$ cup butter,
cut into small pieces

1 tbsp water

FILLING:
3 eggs
150 ml /^{1}/$_4$ pint/^{2}/$_3$ cup single
(light) cream
150 ml/^{1}/$_4$ pint/^{2}/$_3$ cup milk

freshly grated nutmeg

TO SERVE:
whipping cream

1 To make the pastry (pie dough), place the flour and sugar in a mixing bowl and rub in the butter.

2 Add the water and mix together until a soft pastry (pie dough) has formed. Wrap and leave to chill in the refrigerator for about 30 minutes.

3 Roll out the dough to form a round slightly larger than a 24 cm/ 9½ inch loose-bottomed quiche/flan tin (pan).

4 Line the tin (pan) with the dough, trimming off the edges. Prick the dough with a fork and leave to chill in the refrigerator for 30 minutes.

5 Line the pastry case (pie shell) with foil and baking beans.

6 Bake the tart in a preheated oven, 190°C/375°F/ Gas Mark 5, for 15 minutes. Remove the foil and baking beans and bake the pastry case

(pie shell) for a further 15 minutes.

7 To make the filling, whisk together the eggs, cream, milk and nutmeg. Pour the filling into the prepared pastry case (pie shell). Transfer the tart to the oven and cook for 25-30 minutes or until just set. Serve with whipping cream, if wished.

Lemon Tart

Serves 8

INGREDIENTS

PASTRY (PIE DOUGH):
150 g/5^1/2 oz/1^1/4 cups plain
    (all-purpose) flour
25 g/1 oz/5 tsp caster
    (superfine) sugar
125 g/4^1/2 oz/1^1/2 cup butter,
    cut into small pieces

1 tbsp water

FILLING:
150 ml/^{1}/4 pint/^{2}/3 cup
    double (heavy) cream
100 g/3^1/2 oz/^{1}/2 cup caster
    (superfine) sugar

4 eggs
grated rind of 3 lemons
12 tbsp lemon juice
icing (confectioners') sugar,
    for dusting

1 To make the pastry (pie dough), place the flour and sugar in a bowl and rub in the butter. Add the water and mix until a soft pastry (pie dough) has formed. Wrap and leave to chill for 30 minutes.

2 On a lightly floured surface, roll out the dough and line a 24 cm/ 9½ inch loose-bottomed quiche/flan tin (pan). Prick the pastry (pie dough) with a fork and leave to chill for 30 minutes.

3 Line the pastry case (pie shell) with foil and baking beans and bake in a preheated oven, 190°C/ 375°F/ Gas Mark 5, for 15 minutes. Remove the foil and beans and cook for a further 15 minutes.

4 To make the filling, whisk the cream, sugar, eggs, lemon rind and juice together. Place the pastry case (pie shell), still in its tin (pan), on a baking tray (cookie sheet) and pour in the filling.

5 Bake in the oven for about 20 minutes or until just set. Leave to cool, then lightly dust with icing (confectioners') sugar before serving.

Orange Tart

Serves 6-8

INGREDIENTS

PASTRY (PIE DOUGH):
150 g/5 oz/1¼ cups plain (all-purpose) flour
25 g/1 oz/5 tsp caster (superfine) sugar
125 g /4½ oz/½ cup butter, cut into small pieces
1 tbsp water

FILLING:
grated rind of 2 oranges
9 tbsp orange juice
50 g/1¾ oz/⅞ cups fresh white breadcrumbs
2 tbsp lemon juice
150 ml/¼ pint/⅔ cup single (light) cream

50 g/1¾ oz/¼ cup butter
50 g/1¾ oz/¼ cup caster (superfine) sugar
2 eggs, separated
pinch of salt

1 To make the pastry (pie dough), place the flour and sugar in a bowl and rub in the butter. Add the cold water and work the mixture together until a soft pastry (pie dough) has formed. Wrap and leave to chill for 30 minutes.

2 Roll out the dough and line a 24 cm/9½ inch loose-bottomed quiche/flan tin (pan). Prick the pastry (pie dough) with a fork and chill for 30 minutes.

3 Line the pastry case (pie shell) with foil and baking beans and bake in a preheated oven, 190°C/375°F/ Gas Mark 5, for 15 minutes. Remove the foil and beans and cook for 15 minutes.

4 To make the filling, mix the orange rind, orange juice and breadcrumbs in a bowl. Stir in the lemon juice and cream. Melt the butter and sugar over a low heat. Remove the pan from

the heat, add the 2 egg yolks, salt and breadcrumb mixture and stir.

5 Whisk the egg whites with the salt until they form soft peaks. Fold them into the egg yolk mixture.

6 Pour the filling into the pastry case (pie shell). Bake in a preheated oven, 170°C/325°F/Gas 3, for about 45 minutes or until just set. Leave to cool slightly and serve warm.

Coconut Cream Tart

Serves 6-8

INGREDIENTS

PASTRY (PIE DOUGH):
150 g/5^1/2 oz/1^1/4 cups plain (all-purpose) flour
25 g/1 oz/5 tsp caster (superfine) sugar
125 g/4^1/2 oz/^{1}/2 cup butter, cut into small pieces
1 tbsp water

FILLING:
425 ml/^{3}/4 pint/2 cups milk
125 g /4^1/2 oz creamed coconut
3 egg yolks
125 g/4^1/2 oz/^{1}/2 cup caster (superfine) sugar
50 g/1^3/4 oz/^{1}/2 cup plain (all-purpose) flour, sieved

25 g/1 oz/^{1}/3 cup desiccated (shredded) coconut
25 g/1 oz glacé (candied) pineapple, chopped, plus extra to decorate
2 tbsp rum or pineapple juice
300 ml/^{1}/2 pint/1^1/3 cups whipping cream, whipped, plus extra to decorate

1 Place the flour and sugar in a bowl and rub in the butter. Add the water and work the mixture together until a soft pastry (pie dough) has formed. Wrap and leave to chill for 30 minutes.

2 Roll out the dough and line a 24 cm/9½ inch loose-bottomed quiche/flan tin (pan). Prick the pastry with a fork and leave to chill for 30

minutes. Line the pastry case (pie shell) with foil and baking beans and bake in a preheated oven, 190°C/375°F/Gas 5, for 15 minutes. Remove the foil and beans and cook for a further 15 minutes. Leave to cool.

3 To make the filling, bring the milk and creamed coconut to just below boiling point, stirring to melt the coconut.

4 Whisk the egg yolks with the sugar until fluffy. Whisk in the flour. Add the hot milk, stirring. Return the mixture to the pan and gently heat for 8 minutes until thick, stirring. Leave to cool.

5 Stir in the coconut, pineapple and rum and spread the filling in the pastry case (pie shell). Cover with the whipped cream, decorate and chill.

Pine Kernel (Nut) Tart

Serves 8

INGREDIENTS

PASTRY (PIE DOUGH):
150 g /5 oz/1^1/4 cups plain
   (all-purpose) flour
25 g/1 oz/5 tsp caster
   (superfine) sugar
125 g/4^1/2 oz/^{1}/2 cup butter,
   cut into small pieces

1 tbsp water

FILLING:
350 g/12 oz curd cheese
4 tbsp double (heavy) cream
3 eggs

125 g/4^1/2 oz/^{1}/2 cup caster
   (superfine) sugar
grated rind of 1 orange
100 g/3^1/2 oz pine kernels
   (nuts)

1 To make the pastry (pie dough), place the flour and sugar in a bowl and rub in the butter with your fingers. Add the water and work the mixture together until a soft pastry (pie dough) has formed. Wrap and leave to chill for 30 minutes.

2 On a lightly floured surface, roll out the dough and line a 24 cm/9½ inch loose-bottomed quiche/flan tin (pan). Prick the pastry (pie dough) with a fork and leave to chill for 30 minutes.

3 Line the pastry case (pie shell) with foil and baking beans and bake in a preheated oven, 190°C/375°F/ Gas Mark 5, for 15 minutes. Remove the foil and beans and cook the pastry case (pie shell) for a further 15 minutes.

4 To make the filling, beat together the curd cheese, cream, eggs, sugar, orange rind and half of the pine kernels (nuts). Pour the filling into the pastry case (pie shell) and sprinkle over the remaining pine kernels (nuts).

5 Bake in the oven at 170°C/325°F/Gas Mark 3 for 35 minutes or until just set. Leave to cool before serving.

Mixed (Candied) Peel & Nut Tart

Serves 8

INGREDIENTS

PASTRY (PIE DOUGH):
150 g/5^1/2 oz/1^1/4 cups plain
(all-purpose) flour
25 g/1 oz/5 tsp caster
(superfine) sugar
125 g/4^1/2 oz/^{1}/2 cup butter,
cut into small pieces

1 tbsp water

FILLING:
75 g/2^3/4 oz/^{1}/3 cup butter
50 g /1^3/4 oz/ ^{1}/4 cup caster
(superfine) sugar
75 g/2^3/4 oz set honey

200 ml/7 fl oz/1^3/4 cups
double (heavy) cream
1 egg, beaten
200 g/7 oz mixed nuts
200 g/7 oz mixed (candied)
peel

1 To make the pastry (pie dough), place the flour and sugar in a bowl and rub in the butter with your fingers. Add the water and work the mixture together until a soft pastry (pie dough) has formed. Wrap and leave to chill for 30 minutes.

2 On a lightly floured surface, roll out the dough and line a 24 cm/ 9½ inch loose-bottomed quiche/flan tin (pan). Prick the pastry (pie dough) with a fork and leave to chill for 30 minutes.

3 Line the pastry case (pie shell) with foil and baking beans and bake in a preheated oven, 190°C/ 375°F/Gas Mark 5, for 15 minutes. Remove the foil and baking beans and cook for a further 15 minutes.

4 To make the filling, melt the butter, sugar and honey in a small saucepan. Stir in the cream and beaten egg, then add the nuts and mixed (candied) peel. Cook over a low heat for 2 minutes until the mixture is a pale golden colour, stirring constantly.

5 Pour the filling into the pastry case (pie shell) and bake for 15-20 minutes or until just set. Leave to cool, then serve in slices.

Apricot & Cranberry Frangipane Tart

Serves 8-10

INGREDIENTS

PASTRY (PIE DOUGH):
150 g/5^1/2 oz/1^1/4 cups plain (all-purpose) flour
125 g/4^1/2 oz/^{1}/2 cup caster (superfine) sugar
125 g/4^1/2 oz/^{1}/2 cup butter, cut into small pieces
1 tbsp water

FILLING:
200 g/7 oz/1 cup unsalted butter
200g/7 oz/1 cup caster (superfine) sugar
1 egg
2 egg yolks
40 g/1^1/2 oz/6 tbsp plain (all-purpose) flour, sieved (strained)

175 g/6 oz/1^2/3 cups ground almonds
4 tbsp double (heavy) cream
411 g/14^1/2 oz can apricot halves, drained
125 g/4^1/2 oz fresh cranberries

1 Place the flour and sugar in a bowl and rub in the butter. Add the water and work the mixture together until a soft pastry (pie dough) has formed. Wrap and leave to chill for 30 minutes.

2 On a lightly floured surface, roll out the dough and line a 24 cm/ 9^1/2 inch loose-bottomed quiche/flan tin (pan). Prick the pastry (pie dough) with a fork and chill for 30 minutes.

3 Line the pastry case (pie shell) with foil and baking beans and bake in a preheated oven, 190°C/ 375°F/Gas Mark 5, for 15 minutes. Remove the foil and beans and cook for a further 10 minutes.

4 Cream together the butter and sugar until fluffy. Beat in the egg and egg yolks, and stir in the flour, almonds and cream.

5 Place the apricots and cranberries in the pastry case (pie shell) and spoon the filling on top.

6 Bake in the oven for about 1 hour, or until the topping is just set. Leave to cool slightly, then serve warm or cold.

White Chocolate & Almond Tart

Serves 8

INGREDIENTS

PASTRY (PIE DOUGH):
150 g/5 oz/1^1/4 cups plain (all-purpose) flour
25 g/1 oz/5 tsp caster (superfine) sugar
125 g/4^1/2 oz/^{1}/2 cup butter, cut into small pieces
1 tbsp water

FILLING:
150 g/5^1/2 oz/^{1}/2 cup golden (light corn) syrup
50 g/1^3/4 oz/10 tsp butter
75 g/2^3/4 oz/^{1}/3 cup soft brown sugar
3 eggs, lightly beaten

100 g/3^1/2 oz/^{1}/2 cup whole blanched almonds, roughly chopped
100 g/3^1/2 oz white chocolate, chopped roughly
cream, to serve (optional)

1 To make the pastry (pie shell), place the flour and sugar in a mixing bowl and rub in the butter with your fingers. Add the water and work the mixture together until a soft pastry (pie dough) has formed. Wrap and leave to chill for 30 minutes.

2 On a lightly floured surface, roll out the dough and line a 24 cm/9½ inch loose-bottomed quiche/flan tin (pan). Prick the pastry (pie dough) with a fork and leave to chill for 30 minutes. Line the pastry case (pie shell) with foil and baking beans and bake in a preheated oven, 190°C/375°F/ Gas Mark 5, for 15 minutes. Remove the foil and baking beans and cook for a further 15 minutes.

3 To make the filling, gently melt the syrup, butter and sugar together in a saucepan. Remove from the heat and leave to cool slightly. Stir in the beaten eggs, almonds and chocolate.

4 Pour the chocolate and nut filling into the prepared pastry case (pie shell) and cook in the oven for 30-35 minutes or until just set. Leave to cool before removing the tart from the tin (pan). Serve with cream, if wished.

Mincemeat & Grape Jalousie

Serves 4

INGREDIENTS

500 g/1lb 2 oz fresh ready-made puff pastry (pie dough)	411 g/14^1/$_2$ oz jar mincemeat 100 g/3^1/$_2$ oz grapes, seeded and halved	1 egg, for glazing demerara (brown crystal) sugar, for sprinkling

1 Lightly grease a baking tray (cookie sheet).

2 On a lightly floured surface, roll out the pastry (pie dough) and cut it into 2 oblongs.

3 Place one pastry (pie dough) oblong on to the prepared baking tray (cookie sheet) and brush the edges with water.

4 Combine the mincemeat and grapes in a bowl. Spread the mixture over the pastry (pie dough) on the baking tray (cookie sheet), leaving a 2.5 cm/1 inch border.

5 Fold the second pastry (pie dough) oblong in half lengthways, and carefully cut a series of parallel lines across the folded edge, leaving a 2.5 cm/1 inch border.

6 Open out the pastry (pie dough) oblong and lay it over the mincemeat. Seal down the edges of the pastry (pie dough) and press together well.

7 Flute and crimp the edges of the pastry (pie dough). Lightly brush with the beaten egg and sprinkle with demerara (brown crystal) sugar.

8 Bake in a preheated oven, 220°C/425°F/Gas 7, for 15 minutes. Lower the heat to 180°C/350°F/Gas Mark 4 and cook for a further 30 minutes until the jalousie is well risen and golden brown. Leave to cool on a wire rack before serving.

COOK'S TIP

For an enhanced festive flavour, stir 2 tbsp sherry into the mincemeat.

Pear Tarts

Makes 6

INGREDIENTS

250 g/9 oz fresh ready-made puff pastry

25 g/1 oz/8 tsp soft brown sugar

25 g/1 oz/6 tsp butter (plus extra for brushing)

1 tbsp stem (candied) ginger, finely chopped

3 pears, peeled, halved and cored

cream, to serve

1 On a lightly floured surface, roll out the pastry (pie dough). Cut out six 10 cm/4 inch rounds.

2 Place the circles on to a large baking tray (cookie sheet) and leave to chill for 30 minutes.

3 Cream together the brown sugar and butter in a small bowl, then stir in the chopped stem (candied) ginger.

4 Prick the pastry circles with a fork and spread a little of the ginger mixture on to each one.

5 Slice the pear halves lengthways, keeping the pears intact at the tip. Fan out the slices slightly.

6 Place a fanned-out pear half on top of each pastry (pie dough) circle. Make small flutes around the edge of the pastry (pie dough) circles and brush each pear half with melted butter.

7 Bake in a preheated oven, 200°C/400°F/Gas Mark 6, for 15-20 minutes until the pastry is well risen and golden. Serve warm with a little cream.

COOK'S TIP

If you prefer, serve these tarts with vanilla ice cream for a delicious dessert.

Crème Brûlée Tarts

Makes 6

INGREDIENTS

PASTRY (PIE DOUGH):
150 g/5 oz/1^1/4 cups plain (all-
    purpose) flour
25 g/1 oz/5 tsp caster
    (superfine) sugar
125 g/4^1/2 oz/^{1}/2 cup butter,
    cut into small pieces.

1 tbsp water

FILLING:
4 egg yolks
50 g/ 1^3/4 oz/9 tsp caster
    (superfine) sugar

400 ml 14 fl oz 1^3/4 cups
    double (heavy) cream
1 tsp vanilla flavouring
    (extract)
demerara (brown crystal)
    sugar, for sprinkling

1 Place the flour and sugar in a bowl and rub in the butter. Add the water and work the mixture together until a soft pastry (pie dough) forms. Wrap and chill for 30 minutes.

2 Roll out the dough to line six 10 cm/4 inch tart tins (pans). Prick the bottom of the pastry (pie dough) with a fork and leave to chill for 20 minutes

3 Line the pastry cases (pie shells) with foil and baking beans and bake in a preheated oven, 190°C/375°F/Gas Mark 5, for 15 minutes. Remove the foil and beans and cook for 10 minutes until crisp and golden. Leave to cool.

4 Beat the egg yolks and sugar until pale. Heat the cream and vanilla until just below boiling point, then add to the egg mixture, whisking constantly.

5 Place the mixture in a pan and bring to just below the boil, stirring until thick. Do not allow to boil or it will curdle.

6 Leave the mixture to cool slightly, then pour it into the tart tins (pans). Leave to cool and then leave to chill overnight.

7 Sprinkle the tarts with the sugar. Place under a preheated hot grill (broiler) for a few minutes. Leave to cool, then chill for 2 hours before serving.

Mini Frangipane Tartlets with Lime

Makes 12

INGREDIENTS

125 g/4^1/2 oz/1 cup plain (all-purpose) flour
100 g/3^1/2 oz/^{1}/3 cup butter, softened
1 tsp grated lime rind
1 tbsp lime juice

50 g/1^3/4 oz/9 tsp caster (superfine) sugar
1 egg
25 g/1 oz/^{1}/4 cup ground almonds

50 g/1^3/4 oz/^{1}/3 cup icing (confectioners') sugar, sieved (strained)
^{1}/2 tbsp water

1 Reserve 5 teaspoons of the flour and 3 teaspoons of the butter and set aside until required.

2 Rub the remaining butter into the remaining flour, until the mixture resembles fine breadcrumbs. Stir in the lime rind, then the lime juice and bring together to form a soft dough.

3 On a lightly floured surface, roll out the dough thinly. Stamp out twelve 7.5 cm/3 inch rounds and line a bun tin (pan).

4 In a bowl, cream together the reserved butter with the caster (superfine) sugar.

5 Mix in the egg, then the ground almonds and the reserved flour.

6 Divide the mixture between the pastry cases (pie shells).

7 Bake in a preheated oven, 200°C/400°F/ Gas Mark 6, for 15 minutes until set and lightly golden. Remove the tartlets from the tin (pan) and leave to cool.

8 Mix the icing (confectioners') sugar with the water. Drizzle a little of the icing over each tartlet and serve.

Breads & Savouries

Freshly baked bread has never been easier to make, especially with the easy-blend yeasts available nowadays. In this chapter 6 g sachets of easy-blend dried yeast have been used as it is easy to obtain, simple to use and gives good results. If you want to use fresh yeast, replace one sachet of easy blend yeast with 25 g/1 oz of fresh yeast. Blend the fresh yeast into the warm liquid and add 1 teaspoon of sugar. Add to the flour and continue as usual.

Always choose a strong white or brown flour for the bread recipes using yeast, it contains a high proportion of gluten, the protein which gives the dough its elasticity. Always knead the dough thoroughly – this can be done in an electric mixer with the dough hook attachment for about 5-8 minutes, but kneading by hand is most enjoyable and allows the cook the pleasure of relieving their aggression and stress upon the dough!

This chapter also includes a selection of savouries to savour, including a tasty selection of pies, pastries and flans to create a whole medley of delicious dishes that can be used as part of a main meal.

Teacakes

Serves 12

INGREDIENTS

---

450 g/1 lb/4 cups strong white
bread flour
1 sachet easy blend dried
yeast
50 g/1³/4 oz/9 tsp caster sugar

1 tsp salt
25 g/1oz/6 tsp butter, cut into
small pieces
300 ml/¹/2 pint/1¹/4 cups
tepid milk

75 g/2³/4 oz luxury dried fruit
mix
honey, for brushing

---

1 Grease several baking
trays (cookie sheets).

2 Sieve (strain) the flour
into a large mixing
bowl. Stir in the dried
yeast, sugar and salt. Rub
in the butter with your
fingers until the mixture
resembles fine
breadcrumbs. Add the
milk and mix all of the
ingredients together to
form a soft dough.

3 Place the dough on a
lightly floured surface
and knead for about
5 minutes (alternatively,

you can knead the dough
with an electric mixer with
a dough hook).

4 Place the dough in a
greased bowl, cover
and leave to rise in a warm
place for about 1-1¹/2 hours
until it has doubled in size.

5 Knead the dough again
for a few minutes and
knead in the fruit. Divide
the dough into 12 rounds
and place on the baking
trays (cookie sheets). Cover
and leave for a further
1 hour or until springy to
the touch.

6 Bake in a preheated
oven, 200°C/400°F/
Gas Mark 6, for 20 minutes.
Brush the teacakes with
honey while still warm.

7 Leave the teacakes to
cool on a wire rack
before serving them split
in half. Spread with butter
and serve.

Cinnamon Swirls

Makes 12

INGREDIENTS

225 g/8 oz/2 cups strong
   white bread flour
^{1}/2 tsp salt
1 sachet easy blend dried
   yeast
25 g/1 oz/6 tsp butter, cut into
   small pieces

1 egg, beaten
125 ml/4 fl oz/^{1}/2 cup warm
   milk
2 tbsp maple syrup

FILLING:
50 g/1^3/4 oz/10 tsp butter,
   softened
2 tsp ground cinnamon
50 g/1^3/4 oz/3 tbsp soft brown
   sugar
50 g/1^3/4 oz/^{1}/3 cup currants

1 Grease a 23 cm/9 inch square baking tin (pan).

2 Sieve (strain) the flour and salt into a mixing bowl. Stir in the dried yeast. Rub in the butter with your fingers until the mixture resembles breadcrumbs. Add the egg and milk and mix everything together to form a dough.

3 Place the dough in a greased bowl, cover and leave in a warm place for about 40 minutes or until doubled in size.

4 Knead the dough for 1 minute to knock it back (punch down), then roll out to a rectangle 30 × 23 cm/12 × 9 inches.

5 To make the filling, cream together the butter, cinnamon and brown sugar until light and fluffy. Spread the filling over the dough, leaving a 2.5 cm/1 inch border. Sprinkle over the currants.

6 Roll up the dough like a swiss roll, starting at a long edge, and press down to seal. Cut the roll into 12 slices. Place them in the tin, cover and leave for 30 minutes.

7 Bake in a preheated oven, 190°C/375°F/ Gas Mark 5, for 20-30 minutes or until well risen. Brush with the syrup and leave to cool slightly before serving.

Cinnamon & Currant Loaf

Makes a 900 g/2 lb loaf

INGREDIENTS

350 g/12 oz/3 cups plain (all-purpose) flour
pinch of salt
1 tbsp baking powder
1 tbsp ground cinnamon

150 g/5^{1}/2 oz/^{2}/3 cup butter, cut into small pieces
125 g/4^{1}/2 oz/^{3}/4 cup soft brown sugar
175 g/6 oz/^{3}/4 cup currants

finely grated rind of 1 orange
5-6 tbsp orange juice
6 tbsp milk
2 eggs, beaten lightly

1 Grease a 900 g/2 lb loaf tin and line the base with baking parchment.

2 Sieve (strain) the flour, salt, baking powder and ground cinnamon into a bowl. Rub in the butter pieces with your fingers until the mixture resembles coarse breadcrumbs.

3 Stir in the sugar, currants and orange rind. Beat the orange juice, milk and eggs together and add to the dry ingredients. Mix well together.

4 Spoon the mixture into the prepared tin. Make a slight dip in the middle of the mixture to help it rise evenly.

5 Bake in a preheated oven, 180°C/350°F/Gas Mark 4, for about 1-1 hour 10 minutes, or until a fine metal skewer inserted into the centre of the loaf comes out clean.

6 Leave the loaf to cool before turning out of the tin. Transfer to a wire rack and leave to cool completely before slicing.

COOK'S TIP

Once you have added the liquid to the dry ingredients, work as quickly as possible because the baking powder is activated by the liquid.

Orange, Banana & Cranberry Loaf

Serves 8-10

INGREDIENTS

175 g/6 oz/1¹/₂ cups self-
  raising flour
¹/₂ tsp baking powder
150 g/5¹/₂ oz/1 cup soft
  brown sugar
2 bananas, mashed

50 g/1³/₄ oz chopped mixed
  peel
25 g/1 oz chopped mixed nuts
50 g/1³/₄ oz dried cranberries
5-6 tbsp orange juice
2 eggs, beaten

150 ml/¹/₄ pint/²/₃ cup
  sunflower oil
75 g/2³/₄ oz icing
  (confectioners') sugar,
  sieved (strained)
grated rind of 1 orange

1 Grease a 900 g/2 lb loaf tin (pan) and line the base with baking parchment.

2 Sieve (strain) the flour and baking powder into a mixing bowl. Stir in the sugar, bananas, chopped mixed peel, nuts and cranberries.

3 Stir the orange juice, eggs and oil together until well combined. Add the mixture to the dry ingredients and mix until well blended. Pour the mixture into the prepared tin (pan).

4 Bake in a preheated oven, 180°C/350°F/Gas Mark 4, for about 1 hour until firm to the touch or until a fine skewer inserted into the centre of the loaf comes out clean.

5 Turn out the loaf and leave it to cool on a wire rack.

6 Mix the icing (confectioners') sugar with a little water and drizzle the icing over the loaf. Sprinkle the orange rind over the top. Leave the icing to set before serving the loaf in slices.

COOK'S TIP

This tea bread will keep for a couple of days. Wrap it carefully and store in a cool, dry place.

Banana & Date Loaf

Serves 6-8

INGREDIENTS

225 g/8 oz/2 cups self-raising flour
100 g/3¹/2 oz/¹/3 cup butter, cut into small pieces
75 g/2³/4 oz/¹/3 cup caster (superfine) sugar

125 g/4¹/2 oz stoned dates, chopped
2 bananas, mashed roughly

2 eggs, beaten lightly
2 tbsp honey

1 Grease a 900 g/2 lb loaf tin (pan) and line the base with baking parchment.

2 Sieve (strain) the flour into a mixing bowl.

3 Rub the butter into the flour with your fingertips until the mixture resembles fine breadcrumbs.

4 Stir the sugar, chopped dates, bananas, beaten eggs and honey into the dry ingredients. Mix together to form a soft dropping consistency.

5 Spoon the mixture into the prepared loaf tin (pan) and level the surface with the back of a knife.

6 Bake in a preheated oven, 160°C/325°F/Gas Mark 3, for about 1 hour or until golden and a fine metal skewer inserted into the centre comes out clean.

7 Leave the loaf to cool in the tin (pan), then transfer to a wire rack.

8 Serve the loaf warm or cold, cut into thick slices.

COOK'S TIP

This tea bread will keep for several days if stored in an airtight container and kept in a cool, dry place.

Crown Loaf

Makes 1 loaf

INGREDIENTS

225 g/8 oz/2 cups strong
  white bread flour
$^1/_2$ tsp salt
1 sachet easy blend dried
  yeast
25 g/1 oz/6 tsp butter, cut into
  small pieces

125 ml/4 fl oz/$^1/_2$ cup tepid
  milk
1 egg, beaten

FILLING:
50 g/1$^3/_4$ oz/10 tsp butter,
  softened
50 g/1$^3/_4$ oz/3 tbsp soft brown
  sugar

25 g/1 oz chopped hazelnuts
25 g/1 oz stem (candied)
  ginger, chopped
50 g/1$^3/_4$ oz mixed (candied)
  peel
1 tbsp rum or brandy
100 g/3$^1/_2$ oz/$^2/_3$ cup icing
  (confectioners') sugar
2 tbsp lemon juice

1 Grease a baking sheet (cookie sheet). Sieve (strain) the flour and salt into a bowl and stir in the yeast. Rub in the butter. Add the milk and egg and mix together to form a dough.

2 Place the dough in a greased bowl, cover and put in a warm place for 40 minutes until doubled in size. Knead for 1 minute then roll out to a rectangle 30 × 23 cm/12 × 9 inches.

3 Cream together the butter and sugar until light and fluffy. Stir in the hazelnuts, ginger, mixed (candied) peel and rum or brandy. Spread the filling over the dough, leaving a 2.5 cm/1 inch border.

4 Roll up the dough from the long edge to form a sausage shape. Cut into 5 cm/2 inch slices and place on the baking tray (cookie sheet) with the slices just touching. Cover and leave to rise in a warm place for 30 minutes.

5 Bake in a preheated oven, 190°C/325°F/ Gas Mark 5, for 20-30 minutes or until golden. Meanwhile, mix the icing sugar with enough lemon juice to form a thin icing.

6 Leave the loaf to cool slightly before drizzling with icing.

Date & Honey Loaf

Makes 1 loaf

INGREDIENTS

250 g/9 oz/1¼ cups strong
white bread flour
75 g/2¾ oz/¼ cup strong
brown bread flour

½ tsp salt
1 sachet easy blend dried
yeast
200 ml/7 fl oz/¾ cup tepid
water

3 tbsp sunflower oil
3 tbsp honey
75 g/2¾ oz dates, chopped
2 tbsp sesame seeds

1 Grease a 900 g/2 lb loaf tin (pan). Sieve (strain) the flours into a large mixing bowl, stir in the salt and dried yeast.

2 Pour in the tepid water, oil and honey. Mix everything together to form a dough.

3 Place the dough on a lightly floured surface and knead for about 5 minutes until smooth.

4 Place the dough in a greased bowl, cover and leave to rise in a warm place for about 1 hour or until doubled in size.

5 Knead in the dates and sesame seeds. Shape the dough and place in the tin (pan).

6 Cover and leave in a warm place for a further 30 minutes or until springy to the touch.

7 Bake in a preheated oven, 220°C/425°F/Gas Mark 7, for 30 minutes or until a hollow sound is heard when the base of the loaf is tapped.

8 Transfer the loaf to a wire rack and leave to cool. Serve cut into thick slices.

VARIATION

Replace the sesame seeds with sunflower seeds for a slightly different texture, if you prefer.

COOK'S TIP

If you cannot find a warm place, sit the bowl over a saucepan of warm water.

Pumpkin Loaf

Serves 6-8

INGREDIENTS

450 g/1 lb pumpkin flesh
125 g/ 4^1/$_2$ oz /^{1}/$_2$ cup butter,
    softened
175 g /6 oz/^{3}/$_4$ cup caster
    (superfine) sugar

2 eggs, beaten
225 g /8 oz/2 cups plain (all-
    purpose) flour, sifted
1^1/$_2$ tsp baking powder
^{1}/$_2$ tsp salt

1 tsp ground mixed spice
    (allspice)
25 g/1 oz pumpkin seeds

1 Grease a 900 g/2 lb loaf tin (pan) with oil.

2 Chop the pumpkin into large pieces and wrap in buttered foil. Cook in a preheated oven, 200°C/400°F/Gas Mark 6, for 30-40 minutes until they are tender.

3 Leave the pumpkin to cool completely before mashing well to make a thick purée.

4 In a bowl, cream the butter and sugar together until light and fluffy. Add the eggs a little at a time.

5 Stir in the pumpkin purée. Fold in the flour, baking powder, salt and mixed spice (allspice).

6 Fold the pumpkin seeds gently through the mixture, then spoon into the loaf tin (pan).

7 Bake in a preheated oven, 160°C/325°F/Gas Mark 3, for 1^1/$_4$-1^1/$_2$ hours or until a skewer inserted into the centre of the loaf comes out clean.

8 Leave the loaf to cool and serve buttered, if wished.

COOK'S TIP

To ensure that the pumpkin purée is dry, place it in a saucepan over a medium heat for a few minutes, stirring frequently, until it is thick.

Tropical Fruit Bread

Makes 1 loaf

INGREDIENTS

350 g/12 oz/3 cups strong
white bread flour
50 g /1 3/4 oz/5 tbsp bran
1/2 tsp salt
1/2 tsp ground ginger
1 sachet easy blend dried
yeast

25 g/1 oz/2 tbsp soft brown
sugar
25 g/1 oz/6 tsp butter, cut into
small pieces
250 ml/9 fl oz/generous 1 cup
tepid water
75 g/2 3/4 oz glacé pineapple,
chopped finely

25 g/1 oz dried mango,
chopped finely
50 g/1 3/4 oz /2/3 cup
desiccated (shredded)
coconut, toasted
1 egg, beaten
2 tbsp coconut shreds

1 Grease a baking sheet (cookie sheet). Sieve (strain) the flour into a large mixing bowl. Stir in the bran, salt, ginger, dried yeast and sugar. Rub in the butter with your fingers, then add the water and mix to form a dough.

2 On a lightly floured surface, knead the dough for about 5-8 minutes or until smooth (alternatively, use an electric mixer with a dough hook). Place the dough in a greased bowl, cover and leave to rise in a warm place until doubled in size.

3 Knead the pineapple, mango and desiccated (shredded) coconut into the dough. Shape into a round and place on the baking tray (cookie sheet). Score the top with the back of a knife. Cover and leave for a further 30 minutes in a warm place.

4 Brush the loaf with the egg and sprinkle with the 2 tbsp coconut. Bake in a preheated oven, 220°C/425°F/Gas Mark 7, for 30 minutes or until golden.

5 Leave the bread to cool on a wire rack before serving.

Citrus Bread

Makes 1 loaf

INGREDIENTS

450 g/1 lb/4 cups strong white
  bread flour
1/2 tsp salt
50 g/1³/4 oz/9 tsp caster
  (superfine) sugar
1 sachet easy blend dried
  yeast

50 g/1³/4 oz/10 tsp butter, cut
  into small pieces
5–6 tbsp orange juice
4 tbsp lemon juice
3–4 tbsp lime juice
150 ml/¹/4 pint/²/3 cup tepid
  water

1 orange
1 lemon
1 lime
2 tbsp runny honey

1 Lightly grease a baking tray (cookie sheet).

2 Sieve (strain) the flour and salt into a mixing bowl. Stir in the sugar and dried yeast.

3 Rub the butter into the mixture using your fingers. Add all of the fruit juices and the water and mix to form a dough.

4 Place the dough on a lightly floured working surface and knead for 5 minutes. Place the dough in a greased bowl, cover and leave to rise in a warm place for 1 hour.

5 Meanwhile, grate the rind of the orange, lemon and lime. Knead the fruit rinds into the dough.

6 Divide the dough into 2 balls, making one slightly bigger than the other.

7 Place the larger ball on the baking tray (cookie sheet) and set the smaller one on top.

8 Push a floured finger through the centre of the dough. Cover and leave to rise for about 40 minutes or until springy to the touch.

9 Bake in a preheated oven, 220°C/425°F/ Gas Mark 7, for 35 minutes. Remove from the oven and glaze with the honey.

Mango Twist Bread

Makes 1 loaf

INGREDIENTS

450 g/1 lb/4 cups strong
  white bread flour
1 tsp salt
1 sachet easy blend dried
  yeast
1 tsp ground ginger
50 g/1³/4 oz/3 tbsp soft brown
  sugar

40 g/1¹/2 oz /9 tsp butter, cut
  into small pieces
1 small mango, peeled, cored
  and puréed
250 ml/9 fl oz/generous 1 cup
  tepid water
2 tbsp runny honey

125 g/4¹/2 oz /²/3 cup
  sultanas (golden raisins)
1 egg, beaten
icing (confectioners') sugar,
  for dusting

1 Grease a baking tray (cookie sheet). Sieve (strain) the flour and salt into a large mixing bowl, stir in the dried yeast, ground ginger and brown sugar. Rub in the butter with your fingers.

2 Stir in the mango purée, water and honey and mix together to form a dough.

3 Place the dough on a lightly floured surface and knead for about 5 minutes until smooth (alternatively, use an electric mixer with a dough hook). Place the dough in a greased bowl, cover and leave to rise in a warm place for about 1 hour until it has doubled in size.

4 Knead in the sultanas (golden raisins) and shape the dough into 2 sausage shapes, each 25 cm/10 inches long. Carefully twist the 2 pieces together and pinch the ends to seal. Place the dough on the baking tray (cookie sheet), cover and leave in a warm place for a further 40 minutes.

5 Brush the loaf with the egg and bake in a preheated oven, 220°C/ 425°F/Gas Mark 7, for 30 minutes or until golden brown. Leave to cool on a wire rack. Dust with icing (confectioners') sugar before serving.

Chocolate Bread

Makes 1 loaf

INGREDIENTS

450 g/1 lb/4 cups strong white bread flour	1 tsp salt	1 tbsp oil
25 g/1 oz/¼ cup cocoa powder	1 sachet easy blend dried yeast	300 ml/½ pint/1⅓ cups tepid water
	25 g/1 oz/6 tsp soft brown sugar	

1 Lightly grease a 900 g/2 lb loaf tin (pan).

2 Sieve (strain) the flour and cocoa powder into a large mixing bowl.

3 Stir in the salt, dried yeast and brown sugar.

4 Pour in the oil together with the tepid water and mix the ingredients together to make a dough.

5 Place the dough on a lightly floured surface and knead for 5 minutes.

6 Place the dough in a greased bowl, cover and leave to rise in a warm place for about 1 hour or until the dough has doubled in size.

7 Knock back (punch down) the dough and shape it into a loaf. Place the dough in the prepared tin (pan), cover and leave to rise in a warm place for a further 30 minutes.

8 Bake in a preheated oven, 200°C/400°F/Gas Mark 6, for 25-30 minutes, or until a hollow sound is heard when the base of the bread is tapped.

9 Transfer the bread to a wire rack and leave to cool. Cut into slices to serve.

COOK'S TIP

This bread can be sliced and spread with butter or it can be lightly toasted.

Soda Bread

Makes 1 loaf

INGREDIENTS

300 g/10^1/$_2$ oz/2^1/$_2$ cups wholemeal (whole wheat) flour	2 tsp baking powder	1 tsp salt
	1 tsp bicarbonate of soda (baking soda)	1 egg, beaten
300 g/10^1/$_2$ oz/2^1/$_2$ cups plain (all-purpose) flour	2 tbsp caster (superfine) sugar	425 ml/15 fl oz/1^3/$_4$ cups natural yogurt

1 Grease and flour a baking tray (cookie sheet).

2 Sieve (strain) the flours, baking powder, bicarbonate of soda (baking soda), sugar and salt into a large bowl.

3 Beat together the egg and yogurt and pour the mixture into the dry ingredients. Combine well to make a soft and sticky dough.

4 On a lightly floured surface, knead the dough for a few minutes until it is smooth, then shape it into a round about 5 cm/2 inches deep.

5 Transfer the dough to the baking tray (cookie sheet). Using a sharp knife, mark a cross shape on the top of the dough.

6 Bake in a preheated oven, 190°C/375°F/ Gas Mark 5, for about 40 minutes or until the bread is golden brown.

7 Transfer the loaf to a wire rack and leave to cool. Cut into slices to serve.

VARIATION

For a fruity version of this soda bread, add 125 g/4^1/$_2$ oz/^{3}/$_4$ cup of raisins to the dry ingredients in step 2.

Spicy Bread

Makes 1 loaf

INGREDIENTS

225 g/8 oz/2 cups self-raising
    flour
100 g/3$^{1}/_{2}$ oz/$^{3}/_{4}$ cup plain
    (all-purpose) flour

1 tsp baking powder
$^{1}/_{4}$ tsp salt
$^{1}/_{4}$ tsp cayenne pepper
2 tsp curry powder

2 tsp poppy seeds
25 g/1 oz/6 tsp butter, cut into
    small pieces
150 ml/$^{1}/_{4}$ pint/$^{2}/_{3}$ cup milk
1 egg, beaten

1 Lightly grease a baking tray (cookie sheet) with butter.

2 Sieve (strain) the self-raising flour and the plain (all-purpose) flour into a mixing bowl along with the baking powder, salt, cayenne pepper, curry powder and poppy seeds.

3 Rub in the butter until everything is well mixed together.

4 Add the milk and the beaten egg and mix to a soft dough.

5 Turn the dough out on to a lightly floured surface, then knead lightly for a few minutes.

6 Shape the dough into a round and mark it with a cross shape in the centre of the top of the dough.

7 Bake in a preheated oven, 190°C/375°F/Gas Mark 5, for 45 minutes.

8 Transfer the bread to a wire rack and leave to cool. Serve in chunks or slices.

COOK'S TIP

If the bread looks as though it is browning too much, cover it with a piece of foil for the remainder of the cooking time.

Chilli Corn Bread

Makes 12 bars

INGREDIENTS

25 g/4 1/2 oz /1 cup plain (all-purpose) flour
125 g/4 1/2 oz polenta
1 tbsp baking powder
1/2 tsp salt

1 green chilli, deseeded and chopped finely
5 spring onions (scallions), chopped finely
2 eggs

142 ml/4 1/2 fl oz/generous 1/2 cup soured cream
125 ml/4 fl oz/1/2 cup sunflower oil

1 Grease a 20 cm/8 inch square cake tin (pan) and line the base with baking parchment.

2 In a large bowl, mix together the flour, polenta, baking powder and salt.

3 Add the finely chopped green chilli and the spring onions (scallions) to the dry ingredients and mix well.

4 In a mixing jug (pitcher), beat the eggs with the soured cream and sunflower oil. Pour the mixture into the bowl of dry ingredients. Mix everything together quickly and thoroughly.

5 Pour the mixture into the prepared cake tin (pan).

6 Bake in a preheated oven, 200°C/ 400°F/ Gas Mark 6, for about 20-25 minutes or until the loaf has risen and is lightly browned.

7 Leave the bread to cool slightly before turning out of the tin (pan). Cut into bars or squares to serve.

VARIATION

Add 125 g/4 1/2 oz of sweetcorn kernels to the mixture in step 3, if you prefer.

Cheese & Potato Bread

Serves 4

INGREDIENTS

225 g/8 oz/2 cups plain (all-purpose) flour
1 tsp salt

$^1\!/_2$ tsp mustard powder
2 tsp baking powder
125 g/4$^1\!/_2$ oz Red Leicester cheese, grated

175 g/6 oz potatoes, cooked and mashed
200 ml/7 fl oz/$^3\!/_4$ cup water
1 tbsp oil

1 Lightly grease a baking tray (cookie sheet).

2 Sieve (strain) the flour, salt, mustard powder and baking powder into a mixing bowl.

3 Reserve 2 tbsp of the grated cheese and stir the rest into the bowl with the cooked and mashed potatoes.

4 Pour in the water and the oil, and stir all the ingredients together (the mixture will be wet at this stage). Mix them all to make a soft dough.

5 Turn out the dough on to a floured surface and shape it into a 20 cm/8 inch round.

6 Place the round on the baking tray (cookie sheet) and mark it into 4 portions with a knife, without cutting through. Sprinkle with the reserved cheese.

7 Bake in a preheated oven, 220°C/425°F/Gas Mark 7, for about 25-30 minutes.

8 Transfer the bread to a wire rack and leave to cool. Serve the bread as fresh as possible.

COOK'S TIP

You can use instant potato mix for this bread, if wished.

VARIATION

Add 50 g /1$^3\!/_4$ oz chopped ham to the mixture in step 3, if you prefer.

Cheese & Ham Loaf

Serves 6

INGREDIENTS

225 g/8 oz/2 cups self-raising
    flour
1 tsp salt
2 tsp baking powder

1 tsp paprika
75 g/2³/4 oz/¹/3 cup butter,
    cut into small pieces
125 g/4¹/2 oz mature (sharp)
    cheese, grated

75 g/ 2³/4 oz smoked ham,
    chopped
2 eggs, beaten
150 ml/¹/4 pint/²/3 cup milk

1 Grease a 450 g/1 lb loaf
tin (pan) and line the
base with baking
parchment.

2 Sieve (strain) the flour,
salt, baking powder
and paprika into a bowl.

3 Rub in the butter with
your fingers until the
mixture resembles fine
breadcrumbs. Stir in the
cheese and ham.

4 Add the beaten eggs
and milk to the dry
ingredients and mix well.

5 Spoon the cheese and
ham mixture into the
prepared loaf tin (pan).

6 Bake in a preheated
oven, 180°C/350°F/Gas
Mark 4, for about 1 hour or
until the loaf is well risen.

7 Leave the bread to cool
in the tin (pan), then
turn out and transfer to a
wire rack to cool slightly.

8 Serve the bread cut
into thick slices.

COOK'S TIP

*This tasty bread is
best eaten on the day it is
made as it does not keep
well for very long.*

VARIATION

*Any grated hard
cheese can be used for this
bread; use a milder one,
if preferred.*

Cheese & Chive Bread

Serves 8

INGREDIENTS
---

225 g/8 oz/2 cups self-raising
    flour
1 tsp salt
1 tsp mustard powder

100 g/3^1/$_2$ oz mature (sharp)
    cheese, grated
2 tbsp chopped fresh chives
1 egg, beaten

25 g/1 oz/6 tsp butter, melted
150 ml/^{1}/$_4$ pint/^{2}/$_3$ cup milk

---

1 Grease a 23 cm/9 inch square cake tin (pan) and line the base with baking parchment.

2 Sieve (strain) the flour, salt and mustard powder into a large mixing bowl.

3 Reserve 3 tbsp of the grated mature (sharp) cheese for sprinkling over the top of the loaf before baking in the oven.

4 Stir the remaining cheese into the bowl along with the chopped fresh chives. Mix well.

5 Add the beaten egg, melted butter and milk and stir the mixture thoroughly.

6 Pour the mixture into the prepared tin (pan) and spread with a knife. Sprinkle over the reserved grated cheese.

7 Bake in a preheated oven, 190°C/375°F/Gas Mark 5, for 30 minutes.

8 Leave the bread to cool slightly in the tin (pan). Turn out on to a wire rack to cool further. Cut into triangles to serve.

COOK'S TIP

You can use any hard mature (sharp) cheese of your choice for this recipe.

Garlic Bread Rolls

Makes 8

INGREDIENTS

12 cloves garlic	1 tsp salt	1 egg, beaten
350 ml/12 floz/1^1/$_2$ cups milk	1 sachet easy blend dried	milk, for brushing
450 g/1 lb/4 cups strong white	yeast	rock salt, for sprinkling
bread flour	1 tbsp dried mixed herbs	
	2 tbsp sunflower oil	

1 Grease a baking tray (cookie sheet). Peel the garlic cloves and then place them in a pan with the milk, bring to the boil and simmer for 15 minutes. Leave to cool slightly, then process in a blender or food processor to purée the garlic.

2 Sieve (strain) the flour and salt into a large mixing bowl and stir in the dried yeast and mixed herbs.

3 Add the garlic-flavoured milk, sunflower oil and beaten egg to the dry ingredients and mix everything to a dough.

4 Place the dough on a lightly floured work surface and knead lightly for a few minutes until smooth and soft.

5 Place the dough in a greased bowl, cover and leave to rise in a warm place for about 1 hour or until doubled in size.

6 Knock back (punch down) the dough by kneading it for 2 minutes.

Shape into 8 rolls and place on the baking tray (cookie sheet). Score the top of each roll with a knife, cover and leave for 15 minutes.

7 Brush the rolls with milk and sprinkle rock salt over the top.

8 Bake in a preheated oven, 220°C/425°F/ Gas Mark 7, for 15-20 minutes.

9 Transfer the rolls to a wire rack and leave to cool before serving.

Mini Focaccia

Makes 4

INGREDIENTS
---

350 g/12 oz/3 cups strong
    white flour
$1/2$ tsp salt
1 sachet easy blend dried
    yeast
2 tbsp olive oil

250 ml/9 fl oz tepid water
100 g/$3^1/2$ oz green or black
    olives, halved

TOPPING:
2 red onions, sliced
2 tbsp olive oil
1 tsp sea salt
1 tbsp thyme leaves

---

1 Lightly oil several baking trays (cookie sheets). Sieve (strain) the flour and salt into a large mixing bowl, then stir in the yeast. Pour in the olive oil and tepid water and mix everything together to form a dough.

2 Turn the dough out on to a lightly floured surface and knead it for about 5 minutes (alternatively, use an electric mixer with a dough hook and knead for 7-8 minutes).

3 Place the dough in a greased bowl, cover and leave in a warm place for about 1-1½ hours until it has doubled in size. Knock back (punch down) the dough by kneading it again for 1-2 minutes.

4 Knead half of the olives into the dough. Divide the dough into quarters and then shape the quarters into rounds. Place them on the baking trays (cookie sheets) and push your fingers into the dough to achieve a dimpled effect.

5 Sprinkle the red onions and remaining olives over the rounds. Drizzle the olive oil over the top and sprinkle each round with the sea salt and thyme leaves. Cover and leave the dough to rise again for 30 minutes.

6 Bake in a preheated oven, 190°C/375°F/ Gas Mark 5, for 20-25 minutes or until the focaccia are well cooked and golden. Transfer to a wire rack and leave to cool before serving.

Sun-dried Tomato Rolls

Makes 8

INGREDIENTS

225 g/8 oz/2 cups strong
white bread flour
$^{1}/_{2}$ tsp salt
1 sachet easy blend dried
yeast

100 g/3$^{1}/_{2}$ oz/$^{1}/_{3}$ cup butter,
melted and cooled slightly
3 tbsp milk, warmed
2 eggs, beaten

50 g/1$^{3}/_{4}$ oz sun-dried
tomatoes, well drained and
chopped finely
milk, for brushing

1 Lightly grease a baking tray (cookie sheet).

2 Sieve (strain) the flour and salt into a large mixing bowl. Stir in the yeast, then pour in the butter, milk and eggs. Mix together to form a dough.

3 Turn the dough on to a lightly floured surface and knead for about 5 minutes (alternatively, use an electric mixer with a dough hook).

4 Place the dough in a greased bowl, cover and leave to rise in a warm place for 1-1½ hours until the dough has doubled in size. Knock back (punch down) the dough by kneading it for a few minutes.

5 Knead the sun-dried tomatoes into the dough, sprinkling the work surface (counter) with extra flour as the tomatoes are quite oily.

6 Divide the dough into 8 balls and place them on to the baking tray (cookie sheet). Cover and leave to rise for about 30 minutes until the rolls have doubled in size.

7 Brush the rolls with milk and bake in a preheated oven, 230°C/450°F/Gas Mark 8, for 10-15 minutes until the rolls are golden brown.

8 Transfer the rolls to a wire rack and leave to cool slightly before serving.

Thyme Crescents

Makes 8

INGREDIENTS

250 g/9 oz fresh ready-made
   puff pastry (pie dough)
100 g/3$^{1}/_{2}$ oz/$^{1}/_{3}$ cup butter,
   softened

1 garlic clove, crushed
1 tsp lemon juice
1 tsp dried thyme

salt and pepper

1 Lightly grease a baking tray (cookie sheet).

2 On a lightly floured surface, roll out the pastry (pie dough) to form a 25 cm/10 inch round and cut into 8 wedges.

3 In a small bowl, mix the softened butter, garlic clove, lemon juice and dried thyme together until soft. Season with salt and pepper to taste.

4 Spread a little of the butter and thyme mixture on to each of the pastry (pie dough) wedges.

5 Carefully roll up each wedge, starting from the wide end.

6 Arrange the crescents on the prepared baking tray (cookie sheet) and chill for 30 minutes.

7 Dampen the baking tray (cookie sheet) with cold water. This will create a steamy atmosphere in the oven while the crescents are baking and help the pastries to rise.

8 Bake in a preheated oven, 200°C/400°F/ Gas Mark 6, for 10-15

minutes until the crescents are well risen and golden.

COOK'S TIP

Dried herbs have a stronger flavour than fresh ones, which makes them perfect for these pastries. The crescents can be made with other dried herbs of your choice, such as rosemary and sage, or mixed herbs.

Cheese & Mustard Scones

Makes 8

INGREDIENTS

225 g/8 oz/2 cups self-raising
    flour
1 tsp baking powder
pinch of salt

50 g/1³/4 oz/10 tsp butter, cut
    into small pieces
125 g/4¹/2 oz mature (sharp)
    cheese, grated
1 tsp mustard powder

150 ml/¹/4 pint/²/3 cup milk
pepper

1 Lightly grease a baking
tray (cookie sheet).

2 Sieve (strain) the flour,
baking powder and salt
into a mixing bowl. Rub in
the butter with your
fingers until the mixture
resembles breadcrumbs.

3 Stir in the grated
cheese, mustard and
enough milk to form a
soft dough.

4 On a lightly floured
surface, knead the
dough very lightly, then
flatten it out with the palm

of your hand to a depth of
about 2.5 cm/1 inch.

5 Cut the dough into
8 wedges with a knife.
Brush each one with a little
milk and sprinkle with
pepper to taste.

6 Bake in a preheated
oven, 220°C/425°F/
Gas Mark 7, for 10–15
minutes until the scones
are golden brown.

7 Transfer the scones to a
wire rack and leave to
cool slightly before serving.

COOK'S TIP

*Scones should be eaten
on the day they are made as
they quickly go stale. Serve
them split in half and spread
with butter.*

Cheese Sables

Makes about 35

INGREDIENTS

150 g/5¹/2 oz/1¹/4 cups plain (all-purpose) flour
150 g/5¹/2 oz mature (sharp) cheese, grated

150 g/5¹/2 oz/²/3 cup butter, cut into small pieces
1 egg yolk

sesame seeds, for sprinkling

1 Lightly grease several baking trays (cookie sheets).

2 Mix the flour and cheese together in a bowl.

3 Add the butter and mix with your fingers until combined.

4 Stir in the egg yolk and mix to form a dough. Wrap the dough and leave to chill in the refrigerator for about 30 minutes.

5 On a lightly floured surface, roll out the cheese dough thinly. Cut out 6 cm/2¹/2 inch rounds, re-rolling the trimmings to make about 35 rounds.

6 Place the rounds on to the prepared baking trays (cookie sheets) and sprinkle the sesame seeds over the top of them.

7 Bake in a preheated oven, 200°C/400°F/ Gas Mark 6, for 20 minutes until the sables are lightly golden.

8 Transfer to a wire rack and leave to cool slightly before serving.

COOK'S TIP

Cut out any shape you like for your savoury biscuits. Children will enjoy them cut into animal or other fun shapes.

Savoury Curried Biscuits

Makes 40

INGREDIENTS

100 g/3¹/₂ oz/³/₄ cup plain
  (all-purpose) flour
1 tsp salt
2 tsp curry powder

100 g/3¹/₂ oz Cheshire cheese
  (mellow hard cheese),
  grated
100 g/3¹/₂ oz Parmesan
  cheese, grated

100 g/3¹/₂ oz/¹/₃ cup butter,
  softened

1 Lightly grease about 4 baking trays (cookie sheets).

2 Sieve (strain) the plain (all-purpose) flour and salt into a mixing bowl.

3 Stir in the curry powder and the grated Cheshire and Parmesan cheeses. Rub in the softened butter with your fingers until the mixture comes together to form a soft dough.

4 On a lightly floured surface, roll out the dough thinly to form a rectangle.

5 Using a 5 cm/2 inch biscuit cutter, cut out 40 round biscuits (cookies).

6 Arrange the biscuits on the baking trays (cookie sheets).

7 Bake in a preheated oven, 180°C/350°F/Gas Mark 4, for 10–15 minutes.

8 Leave the biscuits to cool slightly on the baking trays (cookie sheets). Transfer the biscuits to a wire rack until completely cold and crisp, then serve.

COOK'S TIP

These biscuits can be stored for several days in an airtight tin or plastic container.

Cheese Pudding

Serves 4

INGREDIENTS

150 g/5^1/2 oz/2^1/2 cups fresh
white breadcrumbs
100 g/3^1/2 oz Gruyère cheese,
grated

150 ml/^{1}/4 pint/^{2}/3 cup tepid
milk
125 g/4^1/2 oz/^{1}/2 cup butter,
melted
2 eggs, separated

salt and pepper
2 tbsp chopped fresh parsley

1 Grease a 2 pint/1 litre/ 4 cup ovenproof dish.

2 Place the breadcrumbs and cheese in a bowl and mix.

3 Pour the milk over the cheese and breadcrumb mixture and stir to mix. Add the melted butter, egg yolks, salt and pepper to taste and parsley. Mix well.

4 Whisk the egg whites until firm. Fold the cheese mixture into the egg whites.

5 Transfer the mixture to the prepared ovenproof dish.

6 Bake the pudding in a preheated oven, 190°C/375°F/Gas Mark 5, for about 45 minutes or until golden and slightly risen, and a fine skewer inserted into the middle of the pudding comes out clean.

7 Serve the cheese pudding hot, with a green salad.

VARIATION

Any strongly flavoured cheese of your choice can be used instead of the Gruyère to make this tasty savoury pudding.

COOK'S TIP

For a slightly healthier alternative, make the cheese pudding with fresh wholemeal (whole wheat) breadcrumbs instead of white ones.

Cheese & Onion Pies

Makes 4

INGREDIENTS

3 tbsp vegetable oil
4 onions, peeled and sliced
   finely
4 garlic cloves, crushed
4 tbsp finely chopped fresh
   parsley

75 g/2³/4 oz mature (sharp)
   cheese, grated
salt and pepper

PASTRY (PIE DOUGH):
175 g/6 oz/1¹/2 cups plain
   (all-purpose) flour
¹/2 tsp salt
100 g/3¹/2 oz/¹/3 cup butter,
   cut into small pieces
3-4 tbsp water

1 Heat the oil in a frying pan (skillet). Add the onions and garlic and fry for 10-15 minutes or until the onions are soft. Remove the pan from the heat and stir in the parsley and cheese and season.

2 To make the pastry (pie dough), sieve (strain) the flour and salt into a mixing bowl and rub in the butter until the mixture resembles breadcrumbs. Stir in the water and mix to a dough.

3 On a lightly floured surface, roll out the dough and divide it into 8 portions.

4 Roll out each portion to a 10 cm/4 inch round and use half of the rounds to line 4 individual tart tins (pans).

5 Fill each round with a quarter of the onion mixture. Cover with the remaining 4 pastry (pie dough) rounds. Make a slit in the top of each tart with

the point of a knife and seal the edges with the back of a teaspoon.

6 Bake in a preheated oven, 220°C/425°F/Gas Mark 7, for 20 minutes. Serve hot or cold.

COOK'S TIP

You can prepare the onion filling in advance and store it in the refrigerator.

Red Onion Tart Tatin

Serves 4

INGREDIENTS

50 g/1¾ oz/10 tsp butter
25 g/1oz/6 tsp sugar
500 g/1 lb 2 oz red onions,
    peeled and quartered

3 tbsp red wine vinegar
2 tbsp fresh thyme leaves
250 g/8 oz fresh ready-made
    puff pastry (pie dough)

salt and pepper

1 Place the butter and sugar in a 23 cm/9 inch ovenproof frying pan (skillet) and cook over a medium heat until melted.

2 Add the red onion quarters and sweat them over a low heat for 10-15 minutes until golden, stirring occasionally.

3 Add the red wine vinegar and thyme leaves to the pan. Season with salt and pepper to taste, then simmer over a medium heat until the liquid has reduced and the red onion pieces are coated in the buttery sauce.

4 On a lightly floured surface, roll out the pastry (pie dough) to a circle slightly larger than the frying pan (skillet).

5 Place the pastry (pie dough) over the onion mixture and press down, tucking in the edges to seal the pastry (pie dough).

6 Bake in a preheated oven, 180°C/350°F/Gas Mark 4, for 20-25 minutes. Leave the tart to stand for 10 minutes.

7 To turn out, place a serving plate over the frying pan (skillet) and carefully invert them both so that the pastry (pie dough) becomes the base of the tart. Serve warm.

VARIATION

Replace the red onions with shallots, leaving them whole, if you prefer.

Puff Potato Pie

Serves 6

INGREDIENTS

750 g/1 lb 9 oz potatoes,
    peeled and sliced thinly
2 spring onions (scallions),
    chopped finely

1 red onion, chopped finely
150 ml/$^1/_4$ pint/$^2/_3$ cup
    double (heavy) cream

500 g/1 lb 2 oz fresh ready-
    made puff pastry (pie
    dough)
2 eggs, beaten
salt and pepper

1 Lightly grease a baking tray (cookie sheet). Bring a saucepan of water to the boil, add the sliced potatoes, bring back to the boil and then simmer for a few minutes. Drain the potato slices and leave to cool. Dry off any excess moisture with paper towels.

2 In a bowl, mix together the spring onions (scallions), red onion and the cooled potato slices. Stir in 2 tbsp of the cream and plenty of seasoning.

3 Divide the pastry (pie dough) in half and roll out one piece to a 23 cm/9 inch round. Roll the remaining pastry (pie dough) to a 25 cm/10 inch round.

4 Place the smaller circle on to the baking tray (cookie sheet) and top with the potato mixture, leaving a 2.5 cm/1 inch border. Brush this border with a little of the beaten egg.

5 Top with the larger circle of pastry (pie dough), seal well and crimp the edges of the pastry (pie dough). Cut a steam vent in the middle of the pastry (pie dough) and, using the back of a knife, mark with a pattern. Brush with the beaten egg and bake in a preheated oven, 200°C/400°F/Gas Mark 6, for 30 minutes.

6 Mix the remaining beaten egg with the rest of the cream and pour into the pie through the steam vent. Return to the oven for 15 minutes, then leave to cool for 30 minutes. Serve warm or cold.

Fresh Tomato Tarts

Serves 6

INGREDIENTS

250 g/9 oz fresh ready-made
    puff pastry (pie dough)
1 egg, beaten
2 tbsp pesto

6 plum tomatoes, sliced
salt and pepper

fresh thyme leaves, to garnish
    (optional)

1 On a lightly floured surface, roll out the pastry (pie dough) to a rectangle measuring 30 × 25 cm/12 × 10 inches.

2 Cut the rectangle in half and divide each half into 3 pieces to make 6 even-sized rectangles. Leave to chill for 20 minutes.

3 Lightly score the edges of the pastry (pie dough) rectangles and brush with the beaten egg.

4 Spread the pesto over the rectangles, dividing it equally between them, leaving a 2½ cm/1 inch border on each one.

5 Arrange the tomato slices along the centre of each rectangle on top of the pesto.

6 Season well with salt and pepper to taste and lightly sprinkle with fresh thyme leaves, if using.

7 Bake the tarts in a preheated oven, 200°C/400°F/Gas Mark 6, for about 15-20 minutes until well risen and golden brown.

8 Transfer the tomato tarts to warm serving plates straight from the oven and serve while they are still piping hot.

VARIATION

Instead of individual tarts, roll the pastry (pie dough) out to form 1 large rectangle. Spoon over the pesto and arrange the tomatoes over the top.

Provençal Tart

Serves 6-8

INGREDIENTS

250 g/9 oz ready-made fresh
    puff pastry (pie dough)
3 tbsp olive oil
2 red (bell) peppers, seeded
    and diced

2 green (bell) peppers, seeded
    and diced
150 ml/^{1}/4 pint/^{2}/3 cup double
    (heavy) cream

1 egg
2 courgettes (zucchini), sliced
salt and pepper

1 Roll out the pastry (pie dough) on a lightly floured surface and line a 20 cm/8 inch loose-bottomed quiche/flan tin (pan). Leave to chill in the refrigerator for 20 minutes.

2 Meanwhile, heat 2 tbsp of the olive oil in a pan and fry the (bell) peppers for about 8 minutes until softened, stirring frequently.

3 Whisk the double (heavy) cream and egg together in a bowl and season to taste with salt and pepper. Stir in the cooked (bell) peppers.

4 Heat the remaining oil in a pan and fry the courgette (zucchini) slices for 4-5 minutes until lightly browned.

5 Pour the egg and (bell) pepper mixture into the pastry case (pie shell).

6 Arrange the courgette (zucchini) slices around the edge of the tart.

7 Bake in a preheated oven, 180°C/350°F/ Gas Mark 4, for 35-40 minutes or until just set and golden brown.

COOK'S TIP

This recipe could be used to make 6 individual tarts – use 15 × 10 cm/6 × 4 inch tins (pans) and bake them for 20 minutes.

Celery & Onion Pies

Makes 12

INGREDIENTS

PASTRY (PIE DOUGH):
125 g/4^1/$_2$ oz/1 cup plain (all-
    purpose) flour
^{1}/$_2$ tsp salt
25 g/1 oz/6 tsp butter, cut into
    small pieces

25 g/1 oz mature (sharp)
    cheese, grated
3-4 tbsp water

FILLING:
50 g/1^3/$_4$ oz/10 tsp butter
125 g/4^1/$_2$ oz celery, chopped
    finely

2 garlic cloves, crushed
1 small onion, chopped finely
1 tbsp plain (all-purpose) flour
50 ml/2 fl oz/^{1}/$_4$ cup milk
salt
pinch of cayenne pepper

1 To make the filling, melt the butter, add the celery, garlic and onion and fry for 5 minutes or until softened.

2 Remove from the heat and stir in the flour, then the milk. Heat gently until the mixture is thick, stirring freqently. Season with salt and cayenne pepper. Leave to cool.

3 To make the pastry, sieve (strain) the flour and salt into a mixing bowl and rub in the butter with your fingers. Stir the cheese into the mixture together with the cold water and mix to form a dough.

4 Roll out three quarters of the dough and using a 6 cm/2½ inch biscuit (cookie) cutter, cut out 12 rounds. Line a patty tin (pan) with the rounds.

5 Divide the filling between the rounds.

Roll out the remaining dough and, using a 5 cm/2 inch cutter, cut out 12 circles. Place the circles on top of the pies and seal. Make a slit in each pie and chill them for 30 minutes.

6 Bake in a preheated oven, 220°C/425°F/ Gas Mark 7, for about 15-20 minutes. Leave to cool in the tin (pan) for about 10 minutes before turning out. Serve warm.

Asparagus & Goat's Cheese Tart

Serves 6

INGREDIENTS

250 g/9 oz fresh ready-made
   shortcrust pastry (pie
   dough)
250 g/9 oz asparagus
1 tbsp vegetable oil

1 red onion, chopped finely
200 g/7 oz goat's cheese
25 g/1 oz hazelnuts, chopped

2 eggs, beaten
4 tbsp single (light) cream
salt and pepper

1 On a lightly floured surface, roll out the pastry (pie dough) and line a 24 cm/9½ inch loose-bottomed quiche/flan tin (pan). Prick the base of the pastry (pie dough) with a fork and leave to chill for 30 minutes.

2 Line the pastry case (pie shell) with foil and baking beans and bake in a preheated oven, 190°C/375°F/Gas Mark 7, for about 15 minutes.

3 Remove the foil and baking beans and return the pastry case (pie shell) to the oven for a further 15 minutes.

4 Cook the asparagus in boiling water for 2-3 minutes, drain and cut into bite-size pieces.

5 Heat the oil in a small frying pan (skillet) and fry the onion until soft. Spoon the asparagus, onion and hazelnuts into the prepared pastry case (pie shell).

6 Process the cheese, eggs and cream in a blender until smooth, or beat by hand. Season well, then pour the mixture over the asparagus, onion and hazelnuts.

7 Bake in the oven for 15-20 minutes or until the cheese filling is just set. Serve warm or cold.

VARIATION

Omit the hazelnuts and sprinkle Parmesan cheese over the top of the tart just before cooking in the oven, if you prefer.

Onion Tart

Serves 6

INGREDIENTS

250 g/9 oz fresh ready-made
shortcrust pastry (pie
dough)
40 g/1^1/$_2$ oz/8 tsp butter
75 g/2^3/$_4$ oz bacon, chopped

700 g/1lb 9 oz onions, peeled
and sliced thinly
2 eggs, beaten
50 g/1^3/$_4$ oz Parmesan cheese,
grated

1 tsp dried sage
salt and pepper

1 Roll out the pastry
(pie dough) on a
lightly floured work
surface (counter) and line
a 24 cm/9^1/$_2$ inch loose-
bottomed quiche/flan
tin (pan).

2 Prick the base of the
pastry (pie dough)
with a fork and leave to
chill for 30 minutes.

3 Heat the butter in a
saucepan, add the
chopped bacon and sliced
onions and sweat them
over a low heat for about
25 minutes until tender.

If the onion slices start to
brown, add 1 tbsp water to
the saucepan.

4 Add the beaten eggs to
the onion mixture and
stir in the cheese, sage and
salt and pepper to taste.
Mix well to combine all
the ingredients.

5 Spoon the onion
mixture into the
prepared pastry case
(pie shell).

6 Bake in a preheated
oven, 180°C/350°F/
Gas Mark 4, for about

20-30 minutes or until the
tart has just set.

7 Leave to cool slightly
in the tin (pan). Serve
the tart warm or cold.

VARIATION

*For a vegetarian version of
this tart, replace the bacon
with the same amount of
chopped mushrooms.*

Pissaladière

Serves 8

INGREDIENTS

4 tbsp olive oil
700 g/1 lb 9 oz red onions,
    sliced thinly
2 garlic cloves, crushed
2 tsp caster (superfine) sugar

2 tbsp red wine vinegar
350 g/12 oz fresh ready-made
    puff pastry (pie dough)
salt and pepper

TOPPING:
2 x 50 g/1³⁄₄ oz cans anchovy
    fillets
12 green stoned (pitted) olives
1 tsp dried marjoram

1 Lightly grease a swiss roll tin (pan). Heat the olive oil in a large saucepan. Add the onions and garlic and cook over a low heat for about 30 minutes, stirring occasionally.

2 Add the sugar and red wine vinegar to the pan and season with plenty of salt and pepper.

3 On a lightly floured surface, roll out the pastry (pie dough) to a rectangle 33 × 23 cm/ 13 × 9 inches. Place the

pastry (pie dough) rectangle on to the prepared tin (pan), pushing the pastry (pie dough) well into the corners of the tin (pan).

4 Spread the onion mixture over the pastry (pie dough).

5 Arrange the anchovy fillets and green olives on top, then sprinkle with the marjoram.

6 Bake in a preheated oven, 220°C/425°F/ Gas Mark 7, for about 20-25 minutes until the

pissaladière is lightly golden. Serve piping hot, straight from the oven.

VARIATION

Cut the pissaladière into squares or triangles for easy finger food at a party or barbecue (grill).

Mini Cheese & Onion Tarts

Serves 12

INGREDIENTS

PASTRY (PIE DOUGH):
100 g/4^1/$_2$ oz/1 cup plain (all-
    purpose) flour
^{1}/$_4$ tsp salt
75 g/2^3/$_4$ oz/^{1}/$_3$ cup butter,
    cut into small pieces
1-2 tbsp water

FILLING:
1 egg, beaten
100 ml/3^1/$_2$ fl oz/generous
    ^{1}/$_3$ cup single (light) cream
50 g/1^3/$_4$ oz Red Leicester
    cheese, grated

3 spring onions (scallions),
    chopped finely
salt
cayenne pepper

1 To make the pastry
(pie dough), sieve
(strain) the flour and salt
into a mixing bowl. Rub in
the butter with your
fingers until the mixture
resembles breadcrumbs.
Stir in the water and mix to
form a dough.

2 Roll out the pastry (pie
dough) on to a lightly
floured surface. Using a
7.5 cm/3 inch biscuit cutter,
stamp out 12 rounds from
the pastry (pie dough) and
line a patty tin (pan).

3 To make the filling,
whisk together the
beaten egg, single (light)
cream, grated cheese and
chopped spring onions
(scallions) in a mixing
jug (pitcher). Season to
taste with salt and
cayenne pepper.

4 Pour the filling
mixture into the pastry
cases (pie shells) and bake
in a preheated oven,
180°C/350°F/Gas Mark 4,
for about 20-25 minutes or
until the filling is just set.

Serve the mini tarts warm
or cold.

VARIATION

*Top each mini tartlet with
slices of fresh tomato before
baking, if you prefer.*

COOK'S TIP

*If you use 175 g/6 oz of
ready-made shortcrust pastry
(pie dough), these tarts can
be made in minutes.*

Ham & Cheese Lattice Pies

Makes 6

INGREDIENTS

250 g/9 oz fresh ready-made puff pastry (pie dough)	125 g/4¹/₂ oz full fat soft cheese	2 tbsp freshly grated Parmesan cheese
50 g/1³/₄ oz ham, finely chopped	2 tbsp chopped fresh chives	pepper
	1 egg, beaten	

1 Roll out the pastry (pie dough) thinly on to a lightly floured work surface (counter). Cut out 12 rectangles measuring 15 × 5 cm/6 × 2 inches.

2 Place the rectangles on to greased baking trays (cookie sheets) and leave to chill for 30 minutes.

3 Combine the ham, cheese and chives in a small bowl. Season with pepper to taste.

4 Spread the ham and cheese mixture along the centre of 6 of the rectangles, leaving a 2.5 cm/1 inch border around each one. Brush the border with the beaten egg.

5 To make the lattice pattern, fold the remaining rectangles lengthways. Leaving a 2.5 cm/1 inch border, cut vertical lines across one edge of the rectangles.

6 Unfold the rectangles and place them over the rectangles topped with the ham and cheese mixture set on the baking trays (cookie sheets). Seal the pastry (pie dough) edges well and lightly sprinkle with the Parmesan cheese.

7 Bake in a preheated oven, 180°C/350°F/Gas Mark 4, for 15-20 minutes. Serve hot or cold.

COOK'S TIP

These pies can be made in advance, frozen uncooked and baked fresh when required.

Vegetarian Baking

Vegetarian food is not a poor substitute for non-meat eaters, it is delicious and nutritious in its own right. The variety of recipes in this chapter will allow vegetarians and vegans to enjoy baking recipes and to experiment with the fillings and toppings to suit their individuals needs.

Most supermarkets and health food shops stock a variety of products to cater for vegetarians' dietary needs and preferences. Useful products include soya milk, which is sold either in concentrated form which needs diluting, ready-to-drink form, or in powdered form; and cooking fats, including various brands of vegan margarine and numerous white vegetable fats which are ideal for pastries and frying.

Tofu (soya bean curd) is a versatile, whitish, curd-like product, high in protein and cholesterol-free, which can be used in sweet and savoury dishes.

Eggless sponges and toppings such as the ones in this chapter are made by adding extra liquid (usually oil) to the mixture and increasing the amount of raising agent.

Curry Pasties

Serves 4

INGREDIENTS

225 g/8 oz/1³/₄ cups plain
    wholemeal (whole wheat)
    flour
100 g/3¹/₂ oz/¹/₃ cup
    vegetarian margarine, cut
    into small pieces
4 tbsp water

2 tbsp oil
225 g/8 oz diced root
    vegetables (such as
    potatoes, carrots and
    parsnips)
1 small onion, chopped
2 garlic cloves, chopped finely

¹/₂ tsp curry powder
¹/₂ tsp ground turmeric
¹/₂ tsp ground cumin
¹/₂ tsp wholegrain mustard
5 tbsp vegetable stock
soya milk, to glaze

1 Place the flour in a mixing bowl and rub in the vegetarian margarine with your fingertips until the mixture resembles breadcrumbs. Stir in the water and bring together to form a soft dough. Wrap and leave to chill in the refrigerator for 30 minutes.

2 To make the filling, heat the oil in a large saucepan. Add the diced root vegetables, chopped onion and garlic. Fry for 2 minutes, then stir in all of the spices and mustard, turning the vegetables to coat them with the spices. Fry the vegetables for a further 1 minute.

3 Add the stock to the pan and bring to the boil. Cover and simmer for about 20 minutes, stirring occasionally, until the vegetables are tender and the liquid has been absorbed. Leave to cool.

4 Divide the pastry (pie dough) into 4 portions.

Roll each portion into a 15 cm/6 inch round. Place the filling on one half of each round.

5 Brush the edges of each round with soya milk, then fold over and press the edges together to seal. Place on a baking tray (cookie sheet). Bake in a preheated oven, 200°C/400°F/Gas Mark 6, for 25-30 minutes until the pastry is golden brown.

Brazil Nut & Mushroom Pie

Serves 4-6

INGREDIENTS

PASTRY:
225 g/8 oz/1³/4 cups plain
    wholemeal (whole wheat)
    flour
100 g/3¹/2 oz/¹/3 cup vegan
    margarine, cut into small
    pieces
4 tbsp water
soya milk, to glaze

FILLING:
25 g/1oz/6 tsp vegan
    margarine
1 onion, chopped
1 garlic clove, chopped finely
125 g/4¹/2 oz button
    mushrooms, sliced
1 tbsp plain (all-purpose) flour

150 ml/¹/4 pint/²/3 cup
    vegetable stock
1 tbsp tomato purée (paste)
175 g/6 oz brazil nuts,
    chopped
75 g/2³/4 oz fresh wholemeal
    (whole wheat)
    breadcrumbs
2 tbsp chopped fresh parsley
¹/2 tsp pepper

1 To make the pastry, rub the margarine into the flour until it resembles fine breadcrumbs. Stir in the water and bring together to form a dough. Wrap and chill for 30 minutes.

2 Melt the margarine for the filling in a pan, add the onion, garlic and mushrooms and fry for 5 minutes until softened. Add the flour and cook for 1 minute, stirring. Slowly add the stock, stirring until the sauce is smooth and beginning to thicken. Stir in the tomato purée (paste), nuts, breadcrumbs, parsley and pepper. Cool slightly.

3 Roll out two thirds of the pastry (pie dough) and use to line a 20 cm/8 inch loose-bottomed quiche/flan tin (pan). Spread the filling in the pastry case (pie shell). Brush the edges of the pastry (pie dough) with soya milk. Roll out the remaining pastry (pie dough) to fit the top of the pie. Seal the edges, make a slit in the top of the pastry (pie dough) and brush with soya milk.

4 Bake in a preheated oven, 200°C/400°F/Gas Mark 6, for 30-40 minutes until golden brown.

Lentil & Red (Bell) Pepper Flan

Serves 6-8

INGREDIENTS

PASTRY:
225 g/8 oz/1³/4 cups plain
    wholemeal (whole wheat)
    flour
100 g/3¹/2 oz/¹/3 cup vegan
    margarine, cut into small
    pieces
4 tbsp water

FILLING:
175 g/6 oz red lentils, rinsed
300 ml/¹/2 pint/1¹/4 cups
    vegetable stock
15 g/¹/2 oz/3 tsp vegan
    margarine
1 onion, chopped

2 red (bell) peppers, cored,
    seeded and diced
1 tsp yeast extract
1 tbsp tomato purée (paste)
3 tbsp chopped fresh parsley
pepper

1 To make the pastry (pie dough), place the flour in a mixing bowl and rub in the vegan margarine with your fingertips until the mixture resembles fine breadcrumbs. Stir in the water and bring together to form a dough. Wrap and chill for 30 minutes.

2 To make the filling, put the lentils in a pan with the stock, bring to the boil and simmer for 10 minutes until the lentils are tender and can be mashed to a purée.

3 Melt the margarine in a small pan and fry the onion and red (bell) peppers until soft.

4 Add the lentil purée, yeast extract, tomato purée (paste) and parsley. Season with pepper. Mix until well combined.

5 On a lightly floured surface, roll out the dough and line a 24 cm/9½ inch loose-bottomed quiche tin (pan). Prick the base of the pastry (pie dough) with a fork and spoon the lentil mixture into the pastry case (pie shell).

6 Bake in a preheated oven, 200°C/400°F/Gas Mark 6, for 30 minutes until the filling is firm.

Garlic & Sage Bread

Serves 4-6

INGREDIENTS

250 g/9 oz/2¹/₄ cups strong brown bread flour	3 tbsp chopped fresh sage	1 tsp honey
1 sachet easy blend dried yeast	2 tsp sea salt	150 ml /¹/₄ pint/²/₃ cup tepid water
	3 garlic cloves, chopped finely	

1 Grease a baking tray (cookie sheet). Sieve (strain) the flour into a large mixing bowl and stir in the husks remaining in the sieve.

2 Stir in the dried yeast, sage and half of the sea salt. Reserve 1 teaspoon of the chopped garlic for sprinkling and stir the rest into the bowl. Add the honey with the tepid water and mix together to form a dough.

3 Turn the dough out on to a lightly floured surface and knead it for

about 5 minutes (alternatively, use an electric mixer with a dough hook).

4 Place the dough in a greased bowl, cover and leave to rise in a warm place until doubled in size.

5 Knead the dough again for a few minutes, shape it into a circle and place on the baking tray (cookie sheet).

6 Cover and leave to rise for a further 30 minutes or until springy to the touch. Sprinkle with

the rest of the sea salt and garlic.

7 Bake in a preheated oven, 200°C/400°F/ Gas Mark 6, for 25-30 minutes. Leave to cool on a wire rack before serving.

Apricot Slices

Makes 12

INGREDIENTS

PASTRY:
225 g/8 oz/1³/₄ cups
  wholemeal (whole wheat)
  flour
50 g/1³/₄ oz finely ground
  mixed nuts

100 g/3¹/₂ oz/¹/₃ cup vegan
  margarine, cut into small
  pieces
4 tbsp water
soya milk, to glaze

FILLING:
225 g/8 oz dried apricots
grated rind of 1 orange
300 ml/¹/₂ pint/1¹/₃ cups
  apple juice
1 tsp ground cinnamon
50 g/1³/₄ oz/¹/₃ cup raisins

1 Lightly grease a 23 cm/9 inch square cake tin (pan). To make the pastry (pie dough), place the flour and nuts in a mixing bowl and rub in the margarine with your fingers until the mixture resembles breadcrumbs. Stir in the water and bring together to form a dough. Wrap and leave to chill for 30 minutes.

2 To make the filling, place the apricots, orange rind and apple juice in a pan and bring to the boil. Simmer for 30 minutes until the apricots are mushy. Cool slightly, then blend to a purée. Stir in the cinnamon and raisins.

3 Divide the pastry (pie dough) in half, roll out one half and use to line the base of the tin. Spread the apricot purée over the top and brush the edges of the pastry (pie dough) with water. Roll out the rest of the dough to fit over the top of the apricot purée. Press down and seal the edges.

4 Prick the top of the pastry (pie dough) with a fork and brush with soya milk. Bake in a preheated oven, 200°C/400°F/Gas Mark 6, for 20-25 minutes until the pastry is golden. Leave to cool slightly before cutting into 12 bars. Serve warm.

Baked Tofu (Bean Curd) Cheesecake

Serves 6

INGREDIENTS

125 g/4¹/₂ oz digestive
  biscuits (graham crackers),
  crushed
50 g/1³/₄ oz/10 tsp vegan
  margarine, melted
50 g/1³/₄ oz stoned dates,
  chopped

4 tbsp lemon juice
rind of 1 lemon
3 tbsp water
350 g/12 oz or 2 x 285 g
  packets firm tofu (bean
  curd)

150 ml/¹/₄ pint/²/₃ cup apple
  juice
1 banana, mashed
1 tsp vanilla flavouring
  (extract)
1 mango, peeled and chopped

1 Lightly grease an
18 cm/7 inch round
loose-bottomed cake
tin (pan).

2 Mix together the
digestive biscuit
(graham cracker) crumbs
and melted margarine in
a bowl. Press the mixture
into the base of the
prepared tin (pan).

3 Put the chopped dates,
lemon juice, rind and
water into a saucepan and
bring to the boil. Simmer

for 5 minutes until the
dates are soft, then mash
them roughly with a fork.

4 Place the mixture in a
blender or food
processor with the tofu
(bean curd), apple juice,
mashed banana and vanilla
flavouring (extract) and
process until the mixture is
a thick, smooth purée.

5 Pour the tofu (bean
curd) purée into the
prepared biscuit (cracker)
crumb base.

6 Bake in a preheated
oven, 180°C/350°F/
Gas Mark 4, for 30-40
minutes until lightly
golden. Leave to cool in
the tin (pan), then chill
thoroughly before serving.

7 Place the chopped
mango in a blender
and process until smooth.
Serve it as a sauce with the
chilled cheesecake.

Pineapple Upside-down Cake

Serves 6

INGREDIENTS

432 g/15 oz can unsweetened
   pineapple pieces, drained
   and juice reserved
4 tsp cornflour (cornstarch)
50 g/1^3/4 oz/3 tbsp soft brown
   sugar
50 g/1^3/4 oz/10 tsp vegan
   margarine, cut into small
   pieces

125 ml/4 fl oz/^{1}/2 cup water
rind of 1 lemon

SPONGE:
50 ml/2 fl oz/^{1}/4 cup
   sunflower oil
75 g/2^3/4 oz/^{1}/3 cup soft
   brown sugar
150 ml/^{1}/4 pint/^{2}/3 cup water

150 g/5^1/2 oz/1^1/4 cups plain
   (all-purpose) flour
2 tsp baking powder
1 tsp ground cinnamon

1 Grease a deep 18 cm/7 inch cake tin (pan). Mix the reserved juice from the pineapple with the cornflour (cornstarch) until it forms a smooth paste. Put the paste in a saucepan with the sugar, margarine and water and stir over a low heat until the sugar has dissolved. Bring to the boil and simmer for 2-3 minutes until thickened. Leave to cool slightly.

2 To make the sponge, place the oil, sugar and water in a saucepan. Heat gently until the sugar has dissolved; do not allow it to boil. Set aside to cool. Sieve the flour, baking powder and cinnamon into a mixing bowl. Pour over the cooled sugar syrup and beat well to form a batter.

3 Place the pineapple pieces and lemon rind on the bottom of the tin (pan) and pour over 4 tablespoons of the pineapple syrup. Spoon the sponge batter on top.

4 Bake in a preheated oven, 180°C/350°F/ Gas Mark 4, for 35-40 minutes until set and a fine metal skewer inserted into the centre comes out clean. Invert on to a plate, leave to stand for 5 minutes, then remove the tin (pan). Serve with the remaining syrup.

152

Date & Apricot Tart

Serves 6-8

INGREDIENTS

225 g/8 oz/1³/4 cups plain
   wholemeal (whole wheat)
   flour
50 g/1³/4 oz mixed nuts,
   ground
100 g/3¹/2 oz/¹/3 cup vegan
   margarine, cut into small
   pieces

4 tbsp water
225 g/8 oz dried apricots,
   chopped
225 g/8 oz stoned dates,
   chopped
425 ml /³/4 pint/2 cups apple
   juice

1 tsp ground cinnamon
grated rind of 1 lemon
soya custard, to serve
   (optional)

1 Place the flour and ground nuts in a bowl and rub in the margarine until the mixture resembles breadcrumbs. Stir in the water and bring together to form a dough. Wrap the dough and leave to chill for 30 minutes.

2 Meanwhile, place the apricots and dates in a saucepan with the apple juice, cinnamon and lemon rind. Bring to the boil, cover and simmer for 15 minutes until the fruit softens and can be mashed to a purée.

3 Reserve a small ball of pastry (pie dough) for making lattice strips. On a lightly floured surface, roll out the rest of the dough to form a round and use to line a 23 cm/9 inch loose-bottomed quiche tin (pan).

4 Spread the fruit filling over the base of the pastry (pie dough). Roll out the reserved pastry (pie dough) and cut into strips 1 cm/¹/2 inch wide. Cut the strips to fit the tart and twist them across the top of the fruit to form a lattice pattern. Moisten the edges of the strips with water and seal them around the rim.

5 Bake in a preheated oven, 200°/400°F/Gas Mark 6, for 25-30 minutes until golden brown. Cut into slices and serve with soya custard, if using.

Fruit Crumble

Serves 6

INGREDIENTS

6 dessert pears,
1 tbsp stem (candied) ginger,
    chopped
1 tbsp molasses (dark
    muscovado sugar)
2 tbsp orange juice

TOPPING:
175 g/6 oz/1½ cups plain
    (all-purpose) flour
75 g/2¾ oz/⅓ cup
    vegetarian margarine, cut
    into small pieces

25 g/1 oz almonds, flaked
    (slivered)
25 g/1 oz/⅓ cup porridge
    oats
50 g/1¾ oz molasses (dark
    muscovado sugar)

1 Lightly grease a 1 litre/2 pint/4½ cup ovenproof dish.

2 Peel, core and quarter the pears, then cut them into slices. In a bowl, mix together the pears, ginger, molasses (dark muscovado sugar) and orange juice. Spoon the mixture into the prepared dish.

3 To make the crumble topping, sieve (strain) the flour into a mixing bowl and rub in the margarine with your fingers until the mixture resembles fine breadcrumbs. Stir in the flaked (slivered) almonds, porridge oats and molasses (dark muscovado sugar) and mix together well.

4 Sprinkle the crumble topping evenly over the pear and ginger mixture in the dish.

5 Bake in a preheated oven, 190°C/375°F/Gas Mark 5, for 30 minutes until the topping is golden and the fruit tender. Serve.

VARIATION

Stir 1 tsp ground mixed spice (allspice) into the crumble mixture in step 3 for added flavour, if you prefer.

Eggless Sponge

Makes one 20 cm/8 inch cake

INGREDIENTS

225 g/8 oz/1¾ cups self-raising wholemeal (self-rising whole wheat) flour
2 tsp baking powder

175 g/6 oz/¾ cup caster (superfine) sugar
6 tbsp sunflower oil
250 ml/9 fl oz/1 cup water

1 tsp vanilla flavouring (extract)
4 tbsp strawberry or raspberry reduced-sugar spread
caster (superfine) sugar, for dusting

1 Grease two 20 cm/8 inch sandwich cake tins (layer pans) and line them with baking parchment.

2 Sieve (strain) the flour and baking powder into a large mixing bowl, stirring in any bran remaining in the sieve. Stir in the caster (superfine) sugar.

3 Pour in the sunflower oil, water and vanilla flavouring (extract) and mix well for about 1 minute until the mixture is a smooth consistency.

4 Divide the mixture between the prepared tins (pans).

5 Bake in a preheated oven, 180°C/350°F/Gas 4, for 25-30 minutes until the centre springs back when lightly touched. Leave to cool in the tins (pans), then turn out and transfer to a wire rack.

6 To serve, remove the baking parchment and place one of the sponges on to a serving plate. Spread with the jam and place the other sponge on top. Dust with a little caster (superfine) sugar.

VARIATION

Use melted vegan butter or margarine instead of the sunflower oil if you prefer, but allow it to cool before adding it to the dry ingredients in step 3.

Cakes

There is nothing more traditional than afternoon
tea and cakes and this chapter gives a wickedly
extravagant twist to some of those delicious tea-time
classics – full of chocolate, spice and all things nice,
these recipes are a treat to enjoy.

The chapter includes a variety of different cakes
depending on the time you have and the effort you
want to spend. Small cakes include Gingerbread,
Carrot Cake and White Chocolate & Apricot
Squares. These cakes are easier to prepare and cook
than larger ones and, in general, are particular
favourites to have with a cup of coffee.

Cakes such as Almond Cake and
Lemon Syrup Cake are made very quickly using
baking powder, which produces quick, well-risen
cakes for all those with little time to spare.

Other cakes require special ingredients to produce
cakes with that 'little something extra'; look out for
the Olive Oil Fruit & Nut Cake and
Coffee & Almond Streusel Cake.

Olive Oil, Fruit & Nut Cake

Serves 8

INGREDIENTS

225 g/8 oz/2 cups self-raising flour
50 g/1³/₄ oz/9 tsp caster (superfine) sugar

125 ml/4 fl oz/¹/₂ cup milk
4 tbsp orange juice
150 ml/¹/₄ pint/²/₃ cup olive oil

100 g/3¹/₂ oz mixed dried fruit
25 g/1 oz pine kernels (nuts)

1 Grease an 18 cm/7 inch cake tin (pan) and line with baking parchment.

2 Sieve (strain) the flour into a bowl and stir in the caster (superfine) sugar.

3 Make a well in the centre of the dry ingredients and pour in the milk and orange juice. Stir the mixture with a wooden spoon, beating in the flour and sugar.

4 Pour in the olive oil, stirring well so that all of the ingredients are evenly mixed.

5 Stir the mixed dried fruit and pine kernels (nuts) into the mixture and spoon into the prepared tin (pan).

6 Bake in a preheated oven, 180°C/350°F/Gas Mark 4, for about 45 minutes until the cake is golden and firm to the touch.

7 Leave the cake to cool in the tin (pan) for a few minutes, then transfer to a wire rack to cool.

8 Serve the cake warm or cold and cut into slices.

COOK'S TIP

Pine kernels (nuts) are best known as the flavouring ingredient in the classic Italian pesto, but here they give a delicate, slightly resinous flavour to this cake.

Chocolate & Pear Sponge

Serves 6

INGREDIENTS

175 g/6 oz/³/₄ cup butter,
    softened
175 g/6 oz/1 cup soft brown
    sugar
3 eggs, beaten

150 g/5¹/₂ oz/1¹/₄ cups self-
    raising flour
15 g/¹/₂ oz/2 tbsp cocoa
    powder

2 tbsp milk
2 small pears, peeled, cored
    and sliced

1 Grease a 23 cm/8 inch loose-bottomed cake tin (pan) and line the base with baking parchment.

2 In a bowl, cream together the butter and soft brown sugar until pale and fluffy.

3 Gradually add the beaten eggs to the creamed mixture, beating well after each addition.

4 Sieve (strain) the self-raising flour and cocoa powder into the creamed mixture and fold in gently until all of the ingredients are combined.

5 Stir in the milk, then spoon the mixture into the prepared tin (pan). Level the surface with the back of a spoon or a knife.

6 Arrange the pear slices on top of the cake mixture, arranging them in a radiating pattern.

7 Bake in a preheated oven, 180°C/350°F/Gas Mark 4, for about 1 hour until the cake is just firm to the touch.

8 Leave the cake to cool in the tin (pan), then transfer to a wire rack until completely cold before serving.

COOK'S TIP

Serve the cake with melted chocolate drizzled over the top for a delicious dessert.

Caraway Madeira

Serves 8

INGREDIENTS

225 g/8 oz/1 cup butter,
  softened
175 g/6 oz/1 cup soft brown
  sugar
3 eggs, beaten

350 g/12 oz/3 cups self-
  raising flour
1 tbsp caraway seeds

grated rind of 1 lemon
6 tbsp milk
1 or 2 strips of citron peel

1 Grease and line a
900 g/2 lb loaf tin (pan).

2 In a bowl, cream
together the butter and
soft brown sugar until pale
and fluffy.

3 Gradually add the
beaten eggs, beating
well after each addition.

4 Sieve (strain) the flour
into the bowl and
gently fold into the
creamed mixture.

5 Add the caraway seeds,
lemon rind and the
milk and fold in until
thoroughly blended.

6 Spoon the mixture into
the prepared tin (pan)
and level the surface with a
palette knife (spatula).

7 Bake in a preheated
oven, 160°C/325°F/Gas
Mark 3, for 20 minutes.

8 Remove the cake from
the oven, place the
pieces of citron peel on top
of the cake and return it to
the oven for a further
40 minutes or until the
cake is well risen and a fine
skewer inserted into the
centre comes out clean.

9 Leave the cake to cool
in the tin (pan) before
turning out and
transferring to a wire rack
until completely cold.

COOK'S TIP

*Citron peel is available in
the baking section of
supermarkets. If it is
unavailable, you can
substitute it with chopped
mixed peel.*

Clementine Cake

Serves 8

INGREDIENTS

2 clementines
175 g/6 oz/³/4 cup butter,
    softened
175 g/6 oz/³/4 cup caster
    (superfine) sugar

3 eggs, beaten
175 g/6 oz/1¹/2 cups self-
    raising flour
3 tbsp ground almonds
3 tbsp single (light) cream

GLAZE AND TOPPING:
6 tbsp clementine juice
2 tbsp caster (superfine) sugar
3 white sugar cubes, crushed

1 Grease an 18 cm/7 inch round tin (pan) and line the base with baking parchment.

2 Pare the rind from the clementines and chop the rind finely. In a bowl, cream together the butter, sugar and clementine rind until pale and fluffy.

3 Gradually add the beaten eggs to the mixture, beating well after each addition.

4 Gently fold in the self-raising flour followed by the ground almonds and the single (light) cream. Spoon the mixture into the prepared tin (pan).

5 Bake in a preheated oven, 180°C/350°F/ Gas Mark 4, for about 55-60 minutes or until a fine skewer inserted into the centre comes out clean. Leave to cool slightly.

6 To make the glaze, put the clementine juice into a small saucepan with the caster (superfine) sugar. Bring to the boil and simmer for 5 minutes.

7 Drizzle the glaze over the cake until it has been absorbed and sprinkle with the crushed sugar cubes.

COOK'S TIP

If you prefer, chop the rind from the clementines in a food processor or blender together with the sugar in step 2. Tip the mixture into a bowl with the butter and begin to cream the mixture.

Glacé (Candied) Fruit Cake

Serves 8

INGREDIENTS

175 g/6 oz/ ¾ cup butter, softened
175 g/6 oz/ ¾ cup caster (superfine) sugar
3 eggs, beaten

175 g/6 oz self-raising flour, sieved (strained)
25 g/1 oz ground rice
finely grated rind of 1 lemon

4 tbsp lemon juice
125 g/4½ oz/ ⅔ cup glacé (candied) fruits, chopped
icing (confectioners') sugar, for dusting (optional)

1 Lightly grease an 18 cm/7 inch cake tin (pan) and line with baking parchment.

2 In a bowl, whisk together the butter and caster (superfine) sugar until light and fluffy.

3 Add the beaten eggs a little at a time. Fold in the flour and ground rice.

4 Add the grated lemon rind and juice, followed by the chopped glacé fruits. Lightly mix all the ingredients together.

5 Spoon the mixture into the prepared tin (pan) and level the surface with the back of a spoon or a knife.

6 Bake in a preheated oven, 180°C/350°F/Gas Mark 4, for 1-1 hour 10 minutes until well risen or until a fine skewer inserted into the centre of the cake comes out clean.

7 Leave the cake to cool in the tin (pan) for 5 minutes, then turn out on to a wire rack to cool completely.

8 Dust well with icing (confectioners') sugar, if using, before serving.

COOK'S TIP

Wash and dry the glacé (candied) fruits before chopping them. This will prevent the fruits sinking to the bottom of the cake during cooking.

White Chocolate & Apricot Squares

Makes 12 bars

INGREDIENTS

125 g/4¹/2 oz/¹/2 cup butter
175 g/6 oz white chocolate, chopped
4 eggs

125 g/4¹/2 oz/¹/2 cup caster (superfine) sugar
200 g/7 oz/1³/4 cups plain (all-purpose) flour, sieved (strained)

1 tsp baking powder
pinch of salt
100 g/3¹/2 oz ready-to-eat dried apricots, chopped

1 Lightly grease a 20 cm/ 9 inch square cake tin (pan) and line the base with baking parchment.

2 Melt the butter and chocolate in a heatproof bowl set over a saucepan of simmering water. Stir frequently with a wooden spoon until the mixture is smooth and glossy. Remove from the heat and leave the mixture to cool slightly.

3 Beat the eggs and caster (superfine) sugar into the butter and

chocolate mixture until well combined.

4 Fold in the flour, baking powder, salt and chopped dried apricots and mix well.

5 Pour the mixture into the tin (pan) and bake in a preheated oven, 180°C/350°F/Gas Mark 4, for 25–30 minutes.

6 The centre of the cake may not be completely firm, but it will set as it cools. Leave in the tin (pan) to cool.

7 When the cake is completely cold turn it out and slice into bars or squares.

VARIATION

Replace the white chocolate with milk or dark chocolate, if you prefer.

Crunchy Fruit Cake

Serves 8-10

INGREDIENTS

100 g/3¹/₂ oz/¹/₃ cup butter, softened

100g/3¹/₂ oz/¹/₂ cup caster (superfine) sugar

2 eggs, beaten

50 g/1³/₄ oz/¹/₃ cup self-raising flour, sieved (strained)

100 g/3¹/₂ oz/²/₃ cup polenta (cornmeal)

1 tsp baking powder

225 g/8 oz mixed dried fruit

25 g/ 1oz pine kernels (nuts)

grated rind of 1 lemon

4 tbsp lemon juice

2 tbsp milk

1 Grease an 18 cm/7 inch cake tin (pan) and line the base with baking parchment.

2 In a bowl, whisk together the butter and sugar until light and fluffy.

3 Whisk in the beaten eggs a little at a time, whisking well after each addition.

4 Fold the flour, baking powder and polenta (cornmeal) into the mixture until well blended.

5 Stir in the mixed dried fruit, pine kernels (nuts), grated lemon rind, lemon juice and milk.

6 Spoon the mixture into the prepared tin (pan) and level the surface.

7 Bake in a preheated oven, 180°C/350°F/Gas Mark 4, for about 1 hour or until a fine skewer inserted into the centre of the cake comes out clean.

8 Leave the cake to cool in the tin (pan) before turning out.

VARIATION

To give a more crumbly light fruit cake, omit the polenta (cornmeal) and use 150 g/5¹/₂ oz/1¹/₄ cups self-raising flour instead.

Chocolate Slab Cake with Frosting

Serves 10–12

INGREDIENTS

225 g/8 oz/1 cup butter
100 g/3¹/₂ oz dark chocolate,
   chopped
150 ml/¹/₄ pint /²/₃ cup water
300 g/10¹/₂ oz/2¹/₂ cups plain
   (all-purpose) flour

2 tsp baking powder
275 g/9¹/₂ oz/1²/₃ cups soft
   brown sugar
150 ml/¹/₄ pint/²/₃ cup
   soured cream
2 eggs, beaten

FROSTING:
200 g/7 oz dark chocolate
6 tbsp water
3 tbsp single (light) cream
1 tbsp butter, chilled

1 Grease a 33 x 20 cm/ 13 x 8 inch square cake tin (pan) and line the base with baking parchment. In a saucepan, melt the butter and chocolate with the water over a low heat, stirring frequently.

2 Sieve (strain) the flour and baking powder into a mixing bowl and stir in the sugar.

3 Pour the hot chocolate liquid into the bowl and then beat well until evenly mixed. Stir in the soured cream, followed by the eggs.

4 Pour the mixture into the prepared tin (pan) and bake in a preheated oven, 190°C/ 375°F/ Gas Mark 5, for 40–45 minutes.

5 Leave the cake to cool in the tin (pan), then turn it out on to a wire rack. Leave to cool completely.

6 To make the frosting, melt the chocolate with the water in a saucepan over a very low heat, stir in the cream and remove from the heat. Stir in the chilled butter, then pour the frosting over the cooled cake, using a spatula to spread it evenly over the top of the cake.

Chocolate & Almond Torte

Serves 10

INGREDIENTS

225 g/8 oz dark chocolate,
broken into pieces
3 tbsp water
150 g/5¹/2 oz/1 cup soft
brown sugar
175 g/6 oz/³/4 cup butter,
softened

25 g/1 oz/¹/4 cup ground
almonds
3 tbsp self-raising flour
5 eggs, separated
100 g/3¹/2 oz/¹/4 cup
blanched almonds,
chopped finely

icing (confectioners') sugar,
for dusting
double (heavy) cream, to serve
(optional)

1 Grease a 23 cm/9 inch loose-bottomed cake tin (pan) and base line with baking parchment.

2 In a saucepan set over a very low heat, melt the chocolate with the water, stirring until smooth. Add the sugar and stir until dissolved, taking the pan off the heat to prevent it overheating.

3 Add the butter in small amounts until it has melted into the chocolate.

Remove from the heat and lightly stir in the ground almonds and flour. Add the egg yolks one at a time, beating well after each addition.

4 In a large mixing bowl, whisk the egg whites until they stand in soft peaks, then fold them into the chocolate mixture with a metal spoon. Stir in the chopped almonds. Pour the mixture into the tin (pan) and level the surface with a palette knife (spatula).

5 Bake in a preheated oven, 180°C/350°F/ Gas Mark 4, for about 40-45 minutes until well risen and firm (the cake will crack on the surface during cooking).

6 Leave the cake to cool in the tin (pan) for 30-40 minutes, then turn it out on to a wire rack to cool completely. Dust with icing (confectioners') sugar and serve in slices with double (heavy) cream, if using.

Carrot Cake

Makes 12 bars

INGREDIENTS

125 g/4¹/2 oz/1 cup self-
raising flour
pinch of salt
1 tsp ground cinnamon
125 g/4¹/2 oz/³/4 cup soft
brown sugar
2 eggs
100 ml/3¹/2 fl oz/scant ¹/2 cup
sunflower oil

125 g/4¹/2 oz carrot, peeled
and grated finely
25 g/1 oz/¹/3 cup desiccated
(shredded) coconut
25 g/1 oz/¹/3 cup walnuts,
chopped
walnut pieces, for decoration

FROSTING:
50 g/1³/4 oz/10 tsp butter,
softened
50 g/1³/4 oz full fat soft
cheese
225 g/8 oz/1¹/2 cups icing
(confectioners') sugar,
sieved (strained)
1 tsp lemon juice

1 Lightly grease a
20 cm/8 inch square
cake tin (pan) and line with
baking parchment.

2 Sieve (strain) the flour,
salt and ground
cinnamon into a large bowl
and stir in the brown sugar.
Add the eggs and oil to
the dry ingredients and
mix well.

3 Stir in the grated
carrot, desiccated

(shredded) coconut and
chopped walnuts.

4 Pour the mixture into
the prepared tin (pan)
and bake in a preheated
oven, 180°C/350°F/Gas
Mark 4, for 20-25 minutes
or until just firm to the
touch. Leave to cool in the
tin (pan).

5 Meanwhile, make the
cheese frosting. In a
bowl, beat together the

butter, full fat soft cheese,
icing (confectioners')
sugar and lemon juice
until the mixture is fluffy
and creamy.

6 Turn the cake out of
the tin (pan) and cut
into 12 bars or slices.
Spread with the frosting
and then decorate with
walnut pieces.

Lemon Syrup Cake

Serves 8

INGREDIENTS

200 g/7 oz/1³/4 cups plain (all-purpose) flour
2 tsp baking powder
200 g/7 oz/1 cup caster (superfine) sugar
4 eggs

150 ml/¹/4 pint/²/3 cup soured cream
grated rind 1 large lemon
4 tbsp lemon juice
150 ml/¹/4 pint/²/3 cup sunflower oil

SYRUP:
4 tbsp icing (confectioners') sugar
3 tbsp lemon juice

1 Lightly grease a 20 cm/8 inch loose-bottomed round cake tin (pan) and line the base with baking parchment.

2 Sieve (strain) the flour and baking powder into a mixing bowl and stir in the sugar.

3 In a separate bowl, whisk the eggs, soured cream, lemon rind, lemon juice and oil together.

4 Pour the egg mixture into the dry ingredients and mix well until evenly combined.

5 Pour the mixture into the prepared tin (pan) and bake in a preheated oven, 180°C 350°F/Gas Mark 4, for 45-60 minutes until risen and golden brown.

6 To make the syrup, mix together the icing (confectioners') sugar and lemon juice in a small saucepan. Stir over a low heat until just beginning to bubble and turn syrupy.

7 As soon as the cake comes out of the oven prick the surface with a fine skewer, then brush the syrup over the top. Leave the cake to cool completely in the tin (pan) before turning out and serving.

COOK'S TIP

Pricking the surface of the hot cake with a skewer ensures that the syrup seeps right into the cake.

Orange Kugelhopf Cake

Serves 6-8

INGREDIENTS

225 g/8 oz/1 cup butter, softened
225 g/8 oz/1 cup caster (superfine) sugar
4 eggs, separated
425 g/15 oz/3 3/4 cups plain (all-purpose) flour

3 tsp baking powder
pinch of salt
300 ml/1/2 pint/1 1/4 cups fresh orange juice
1 tbsp orange flower water
1 tsp grated orange rind

SYRUP:
200 ml/7 fl oz/3/4 cup orange juice
200 g/7 oz/1 cup granulated sugar

1 Grease and flour a 25 cm/10 inch kugelhopf tin (pan) or deep ring mould (mold).

2 Cream together the butter and caster (superfine) sugar until light. Add the egg yolks one at a time, whisking well after each addition.

3 Sieve (strain) together the flour, salt and baking powder in a bowl. Fold the flour mixture and the orange juice alternately into the creamed mixture. Stir in the orange flower water and orange rind.

4 Whisk the egg whites until they reach the soft peak stage and fold them into the mixture.

5 Pour into the prepared mould (mold) and bake in a preheated oven, 180°C/350°F/Gas Mark 4, for 50-55 minutes or until a metal skewer inserted into the centre of the cake comes out clean.

6 In a saucepan, bring the orange juice and sugar to the boil, then simmer for 5 minutes until the sugar has dissolved.

7 Remove the cake from the oven and leave in the tin (pan) to cool for 10 minutes. Prick the top of the cake with a skewer and brush over half of the syrup. Cool for 10 minutes, then invert on to a wire rack over a deep plate and brush the remaining syrup over the entire cake. Serve.

Coconut Cake

Serves 6-8

INGREDIENTS

225 g/8 oz/ self-raising flour
   (self-rising) flour
pinch of salt
100 g/3^1/2 oz/^{1}/2 cup butter,
   cut into small pieces

100 g/3^1/2 oz/^{1}/2 cup
   demerara (brown crystal)
   sugar
100 g/3^1/2 oz/1 cup desiccated
   (shredded) coconut, plus
   extra for sprinkling

2 eggs, beaten
4 tbsp milk

1 Grease a 900 g/2 lb loaf tin and line the base with baking parchment.

2 Sieve (strain) the flour and salt into a mixing bowl and rub in the butter with your fingers until the mixture resembles fine breadcrumbs.

3 Stir in the sugar, coconut, eggs and milk and mix to a soft dropping consistency.

4 Spoon the mixture into the prepared tin (pan) and level the surface. Bake in a preheated oven, 160°C/325°F/Gas Mark 3, for 30 minutes.

5 Remove the cake from the oven and sprinkle with the reserved coconut. Return the cake to the oven and cook for a further 30 minutes until well risen and golden and a fine skewer inserted into the centre comes out clean.

6 Leave the cake to cool in the tin (pan) before turning out and transferring to a wire rack to cool completely before serving.

COOK'S TIP

The flavour of this cake is enhanced by storing it in a cool dry place for a few days before eating.

Apple Cake with Cider

Makes a 20 cm/8 inch cake

INGREDIENTS

225 g/8 oz/2 cups self-raising
flour
1 tsp baking powder
75 g/2³/4 oz/¹/3 cup butter,
cut into small pieces
75 g/2³/4 oz/¹/3 cup caster
(superfine) sugar

50 g/1³/4 oz dried apple,
chopped
75 g/2³/4 oz/5 tbsp raisins
150 ml/¹/4 pint/²/3 cup sweet
cider

1 egg, beaten
175 g/6 oz raspberries

1 Grease a 20 cm/8 inch cake tin (pan) and line with baking parchment.

2 Sieve (strain) the flour and baking powder into a mixing bowl and rub in the butter with your fingers until the mixture resembles fine breadcrumbs.

3 Stir in the caster (superfine) sugar, chopped dried apple and raisins, and mix well.

4 Pour in the sweet cider and egg and mix together until thoroughly blended. Stir in the raspberries very gently so they do not break up.

5 Pour the mixture into the prepared cake tin (pan).

6 Bake in a preheated oven, 190°C/375°F/ Gas Mark 5, for about 40 minutes until risen and lightly golden. Leave the cake to cool in the tin (pan), then turn out on to a wire rack. Leave until completely cold before serving.

VARIATION

If you don't want to use cider, replace it with clear apple juice, if you prefer.

Spiced Apple Ring

Serves 8

INGREDIENTS
---

175 g/6 oz/³/₄ cup butter, softened

175 g/6 oz/³/₄ cup caster (superfine) sugar

3 eggs, beaten

175 g/6 oz/1¹/₂ cups self-raising flour

1 tsp ground cinnamon

1 tsp ground mixed spice (allspice)

2 dessert apples, cored and grated

2 tbsp apple juice or milk

25 g/1 oz/¹/₄ cup flaked (slivered) almonds

1 Lightly grease a 25 cm/10 inch ovenproof ring mould (mold).

2 In a mixing bowl, cream together the butter and sugar until light and fluffy. Gradually add the beaten eggs, beating well after each addition, until fully incorporated.

3 Sieve (strain) the flour and spices, then carefully fold them into the creamed mixture.

4 Stir in the grated apples and the apple juice or milk and mix to a soft dropping consistency.

5 Sprinkle the almonds around the base of the mould (mold) and spoon the cake mixture on top. Level the surface with the back of the spoon.

6 Bake in a preheated oven, 180°C/350°F/Gas Mark 4, for 30 minutes until well risen and a fine skewer inserted into the centre comes out clean.

7 Leave the cake to cool in the tin (pan) before turning out and transferring to a wire rack to cool completely. Serve the apple ring cut into slices.

COOK'S TIP

This cake can also be made in an 18 cm/7 inch round cake tin (pan) if you do not have an ovenproof ring mould (mold).

Marbled Chocolate Cake

Serves 8

INGREDIENTS

175 g/6 oz/³/4 cup butter,
  softened
175 g/6 oz/³/4 cup caster
  (superfine) sugar

3 eggs, beaten
150 g/5¹/2 oz/1¹/4 cups self-
  raising (self-rising) flour,
  sieved (strained)

25 g/1 oz/¹/4 cup cocoa
  powder, sieved (strained)
5–6 tbsp orange juice
grated rind of 1 orange

1 Lightly grease a 25 cm/
10 inch ovenproof ring
mould (mold).

2 In a mixing bowl,
cream together the
butter and sugar with an
electric whisk for about
5 minutes.

3 Add the beaten egg
a little at a time,
whisking well after each
addition.

4 Fold the flour into the
creamed mixture
carefully, then spoon half
of the mixture into a
separate mixing bowl.

5 Fold the cocoa powder
and half of the orange
juice into one bowl and
mix gently.

6 Fold the orange rind
and remaining orange
juice into the other bowl
and mix gently.

7 Place spoonfuls of each
of the mixtures
alternately into the mould
(mold), then drag a skewer
through the mixture to
create a marbled effect.

8 Bake in a preheated
oven, 180°C/350°F/
Gas Mark 4, for about

30–35 minutes until well
risen and a skewer inserted
into the centre comes
out clean.

9 Leave the cake to cool
in the mould (mold)
before turning out on to a
wire rack.

VARIATION

*For a richer chocolate
flavour, add 40 g/1³/4 oz
chocolate drops to the
cocoa mixture.*

Coffee & Almond Streusel Cake

Serves 8

INGREDIENTS

275 g/9¹/₂ oz/1¹/₄ cups plain
 (all-purpose) flour
1 tbsp baking powder
75 g/2³/₄ oz/¹/₃ cup caster
 (superfine) sugar
150 ml/¹/₄ pint/²/₃ cup milk
2 eggs
100 g/3¹/₂ oz/¹/₂ cup butter,
 melted and cooled

2 tbsp instant coffee mixed
 with 1 tbsp boiling water
50 g/1³/₄ oz/¹/₃ cup almonds,
 chopped
icing (confectioners' sugar),
 for dusting

TOPPING:
75 g/2³/₄ oz/¹/₂ cup self-
 raising flour
75 g/2³/₄ oz/¹/₃ cup demerara
 (brown crystal) sugar
25 g/1 oz/6 tsp butter, cut into
 small pieces
1 tsp ground mixed spice
 (allspice)
1 tbsp water

1 Grease a 23 cm/9 inch loose-bottomed round cake tin (pan) and line with baking parchment. Sieve (strain) together the flour and baking powder into a mixing bowl, then stir in the caster (superfine) sugar.

2 Whisk the milk, eggs, butter and coffee mixture together and pour on to the dry ingredients. Add the chopped almonds and mix lightly together. Spoon the mixture into the tin (pan).

3 To make the topping, mix the flour and demerara (brown crystal) sugar together. Rub in the butter until the mixture is crumbly. Sprinkle in the ground mixed spice (allspice) and the water and bring the mixture together in loose crumbs. Sprinkle the topping over the cake mixture.

4 Bake in a preheated oven, 190°C/375°F/ Gas Mark 5, for 50 minutes-1 hour. Cover loosely with foil if the topping starts to brown too quickly. Leave to cool in the tin (pan), then turn out. Dust with icing (confectioners') sugar just before serving.

Sugar-free Fruit Cake

Serves 8-10

INGREDIENTS

350 g/12 oz/3 cups plain (all-purpose) flour
2 tsp baking powder
1 tsp ground mixed spice (allspice)
125 g/4¹/₂ oz/¹/₂ cup butter, cut into small pieces

75 g/2³/₄ oz ready-to-eat dried apricots, chopped
75 g/2³/₄ oz dates, chopped
75 g/2³/₄ oz/¹/₃ cup glacé (candied) cherries, chopped
100 g/3¹/₂ oz/²/₃ cup raisins
125 ml/4 fl oz/¹/₂ cup milk

2 eggs, beaten
grated rind of 1 orange
5-6 tbsp orange juice
3 tbsp runny honey

1 Grease a 20 cm/8 inch round cake tin (pan) and line the base with baking parchment.

2 Sieve (strain) the flour, baking powder and ground mixed spice (allspice) into a large mixing bowl.

3 Rub in the butter until the mixture resembles fine breadcrumbs.

4 Carefully stir in the apricots, dates, glacé (candied) cherries and raisins with the milk, beaten eggs, grated orange rind and orange juice.

5 Stir in the honey and mix everything together to form a soft dropping consistency. Spoon into the prepared cake tin (pan) and level the surface.

6 Bake in a preheated oven, 180°C/350°F/Gas Mark 4, for 1 hour until a fine skewer inserted into the centre of the cake comes out clean.

7 Leave the cake to cool in the tin (pan) before turning out.

VARIATION

For a fruity alternative, replace the honey with 1 mashed ripe banana, if you prefer.

Almond Cake

Serves 8

INGREDIENTS

100 g/3^1/2 oz/^{1}/3 cup soft tub
   margarine
50 g/1^3/4 oz/3 tbsp soft brown
   sugar
2 eggs
175 g/6 oz/1^1/2 cups self-
   raising flour

1 tsp baking powder
4 tbsp milk
2 tbsp runny honey
50 g/1^3/4 oz/^{1}/2 cup flaked
   almonds

SYRUP:
150 ml/^{1}/4 pint/^{2}/3 cup runny
   honey
2 tbsp lemon juice

1 Grease an 18 cm/7 inch round cake tin (pan) and line with baking parchment.

2 Place the margarine, brown sugar, eggs, flour, baking powder, milk and honey in a large mixing bowl and beat well for about 1 minute until all of the ingredients are thoroughly mixed together.

3 Spoon into the prepared tin (pan), level the surface with the back of a spoon or a knife and sprinkle with the almonds.

4 Bake in a preheated oven, 180°C/350°F/ Gas Mark 4, for about 50 minutes or until the cake is well risen.

5 Meanwhile, make the syrup. Combine the honey and lemon juice in a small saucepan and simmer for about 5 minutes or until the syrup starts to coat the back of a spoon.

6 As soon as the cake comes out of the oven, pour over the syrup, allowing it to seep into the middle of the cake.

7 Leave the cake to cool for at least 2 hours before slicing.

Gingerbread

Makes 12 bars

INGREDIENTS

150 g/5¹/2 oz/²/3 cup butter
175 g/6 oz/1 cup soft brown
    sugar
2 tbsp black treacle (molasses)
225 g/8 oz/2 cups plain (all-
    purpose) flour

1 tsp baking powder
2 tsp bicarbonate of soda
    (baking soda)
2 tsp ground ginger
150 ml/¹/4 pint/²/3 cup milk

1 egg, beaten
2 dessert apples, peeled,
    chopped and coated with
    1 tbsp lemon juice

1 Grease a 23 cm/9 inch square cake tin (pan) and line with baking parchment.

2 Melt the butter, sugar and treacle (molasses) in a pan over a low heat. Leave the mixture to cool.

3 Sieve (strain) the flour, baking powder, bicarbonate of soda (baking soda) and ginger into a mixing bowl.

4 Stir in the milk, beaten egg and cooled buttery liquid, followed by the chopped apples coated with the lemon juice.

5 Mix everything together gently, then pour the mixture into the prepared tin (pan).

6 Bake in a preheated oven, 170°C/325°F/Gas Mark 3, for 30-35 minutes until the cake has risen and a fine skewer inserted into the centre comes out clean.

7 Leave the cake to cool in the tin (pan) before turning out and cutting into 12 bars.

VARIATION

If you enjoy the flavour of ginger, try adding 25 g (1 oz) stem (candied) ginger, chopped finely, to the mixture in step 3.

Apple Shortcakes

Makes 4

INGREDIENTS

150 g/5^1/2 oz/1^1/4 cups plain
(all-purpose) flour
^{1}/2 tsp salt
1 tsp baking powder
1 tbsp caster (superfine) sugar
25 g/1 oz/6 tsp butter, cut into
small pieces
50 ml/2 fl oz/^{1}/4 cup milk

icing (confectioners') sugar,
for dusting

FILLING:
3 dessert apples, peeled, cored
and sliced
100 g/3^1/2 oz/^{1}/2 cup caster
(superfine) sugar

1 tbsp lemon juice
1 tsp ground cinnamon
300 ml/^{1}/2 pint/1^1/3 cups
water
150 ml/^{1}/4 pint/^{2}/3 cup double
(heavy) cream, whipped
lightly

1 Lightly grease a baking tray (cookie sheet).

2 Sieve (strain) the flour, salt and baking powder into a bowl. Stir in the sugar, then rub in the butter until the mixture resembles fine breadcrumbs. Pour in the milk and mix everything to a soft dough.

3 Knead the dough, then roll out to a thickness of 1 cm/^{1}/2 inch. Stamp out 4 rounds, using a

5 cm/2 inch cutter. Transfer the rounds to the prepared baking tray (sheet). Bake in a preheated oven, 220°C/425°F/Gas Mark 7, for about 15 minutes until the shortcakes are well risen and lightly browned. Leave to cool.

4 To make the filling, place the apple slices, sugar, lemon juice and cinnamon in a saucepan. Add the water, bring to the boil and simmer uncovered

for 5-10 minutes until the apples are tender. Leave to cool a little, then remove the apples from the pan.

5 To serve, split the shortcakes in half. Place each bottom half on an individual serving plate and spoon on a quarter of the apple slices, then the cream. Place the other half of the shortcake on top. Serve dusted with icing (confectioners') sugar, if wished.

Treacle Scones

Makes 8

INGREDIENTS

225 g/8 oz/2 cups self-raising flour
1 tbsp caster (superfine) sugar
pinch of salt

75 g/2 ³/4 oz/¹/3 cup butter, cut into small pieces
1 dessert apple, peeled, cored and chopped
1 egg, beaten

2 tbsp black treacle (molasses)
75 ml/2¹/2 fl oz/5 tbsp milk

1 Lightly grease a baking tray (cookie sheet).

2 Sieve (strain) the flour, sugar and salt into a mixing bowl.

3 Rub in the butter with your fingers until the mixture resembles fine breadcrumbs.

4 Stir the chopped apple into the mixture.

5 Mix the beaten egg, treacle (molasses) and milk together in a jug (pitcher). Add to the dry ingredients to form a soft dough.

6 On a lightly floured surface, roll out the dough to 2 cm/³/4 inches thick and cut out 8 scones, using a 5 cm/2 inch cutter.

7 Arrange the scones on the prepared baking tray (cookie sheet) and bake in a preheated oven, 220°C/425°F/Gas Mark 7, for 8-10 minutes.

8 Transfer the scones to a wire rack and leave to cool slightly.

9 Serve split in half and spread with butter.

COOK'S TIP

These scones can be frozen, but are best defrosted and eaten within 1 month.

Cakes

Cherry Scones

Makes 8

INGREDIENTS

225 g/8 oz/2 cups self-raising
   flour
1 tbsp caster (superfine) sugar
pinch of salt

75 g/2³/4 oz/¹/3 cup butter,
   cut into small pieces
40 g/1¹/2 oz/3 tbsp glacé
   (candied) cherries, chopped

40 g/1¹/2 oz/3 tbsp sultanas
   (golden raisins)
1 egg, beaten
50 ml/2 fl oz/¹/4 cup milk

1 Lightly grease a baking tray (cookie sheet).

2 Sieve (strain) the flour, sugar and salt into a mixing bowl and rub in the butter with your fingers until the scone mixture resembles breadcrumbs.

3 Stir in the glacé (candied) cherries and sultanas (golden raisins). Add the beaten egg.

4 Reserve 1 tablespoon of the milk for glazing, then add the remainder to the mixture. Mix together to form a soft dough.

5 On a floured surface, roll out the dough to a thickness of 2 cm/³/4 inches and cut out 8 scones, using a 5 cm/2 inch cutter.

6 Place the scones on to the baking tray (cookie sheet) and brush with the reserved milk.

7 Bake in a preheated oven, 220°C/425°F/Gas Mark 7, for 8-10 minutes or until the scones are golden brown.

8 Leave to cool on a wire rack, then serve split and buttered.

COOK'S TIP

These scones will freeze very successfully but they are best defrosted and eaten within 1 month.

Cranberry Muffins

Makes 18

INGREDIENTS

225 g/8 oz/2 cups plain (all-purpose) flour
2 tsp baking powder
1/2 tsp salt

50 g/1³/4 oz/9 tsp caster (superfine) sugar
50 g/1³/4 oz/10 tsp butter, melted
2 eggs, beaten

200 ml/7 fl oz/³/4 cup milk
100 g/3¹/2 oz fresh cranberries
2 tbsp freshly grated Parmesan cheese

1 Lightly grease 2 bun (patty) tins (pans).

2 Sieve (strain) the flour, baking powder and salt into a mixing bowl. Stir in the caster (superfine) sugar.

3 In a separate bowl, mix the butter, beaten eggs and milk together, then pour into the bowl of dry ingredients.

4 Mix lightly together until all of the ingredients are evenly combined, then stir in the fresh cranberries.

5 Divide the mixture between the prepared tins (pans).

6 Sprinkle the grated Parmesan cheese over the top of each muffin mixture.

7 Bake in a preheated oven, 200°C/400°F/ Gas Mark 6, for about 20 minutes or until the muffins are well risen and a golden brown colour.

8 Leave the muffins to cool in the tins (pans). Transfer the muffins to a wire rack and leave to cool completely before serving.

VARIATION

For a sweet alternative to this recipe, replace the Parmesan cheese with demerara (brown crystal) sugar in step 6, if you prefer.

Biscuits (Cookies)

Nothing can compare with a home-made biscuit (cookie) for bringing a touch of pleasure to a coffee break or tea-time. This selection of delicious biscuits (cookies) and after-dinner treats will tantalise your taste buds and keep you coming back for more.

Moreish biscuits (cookies) like Citrus Crescents, Meringues, White Chocolate Cookies and Gingernuts are quick, easy and satisfying to make. You can easily vary the finished shape of Vanilla Hearts, Caraway Biscuits (Cookies) and Lemon Jumbles if you have a favourite pastry cutter! The possibilities for inventiveness when making biscuits (cookies) are endless.

For biscuit (cookie) making, you need the best ingredients: nuts should be as fresh as possible, use good quality dark and white chocolate, sugars should be unrefined pure cane sugars and you will discover that the best biscuits are made with butter.

Always leave biscuits (cookies) to cool on a wire rack and then store them in an airtight container to keep them fresh.

Spiced Biscuits (Cookies)

Makes about 24

INGREDIENTS

175 g/6 oz/³/4 cup unsalted butter
175 g/6 oz/1 cup dark muscovado sugar
225 g/8 oz/2 cups plain (all-purpose) flour

pinch of salt
¹/2 tsp bicarbonate of soda (baking soda)
1 tsp ground cinnamon
¹/2 tsp ground coriander
¹/2 tsp ground nutmeg

¹/4 tsp ground cloves
2 tbsp dark rum

1 Lightly grease 2 baking trays (cookie sheets).

2 Cream together the butter and sugar in a mixing bowl and whisk until light and fluffy.

3 Sieve (strain) the flour, salt, bicarbonate of soda (baking soda), cinnamon, coriander, nutmeg and cloves into the creamed mixture and combine well.

4 Stir the dark rum into the creamed mixture.

5 Using 2 teaspoons, place small mounds of the mixture, on to the baking trays (cookie sheets), placing them 7 cm/3 inch apart to allow for spreading during cooking. Flatten each one slightly with the back of a spoon.

6 Bake in a preheated oven, 180°C/350°F/Gas Mark 4, for 10-12 minutes until golden.

7 Leave the biscuits (cookies) to cool and crispen on wire racks before serving.

COOK'S TIP

Use the back of a fork to flatten the biscuits (cookies) slightly before baking.

Cinnamon & Sunflower Squares

Makes 12

INGREDIENTS

250 g/9 oz/1 cup butter, softened
250 g/9 oz/1¹/4 cups caster (superfine) sugar
3 eggs, beaten

250 g/9 oz/2 cups self-raising flour
¹/2 tsp bicarbonate of soda (baking soda)

1 tbsp ground cinnamon
150 ml/¹/4 pint/²/3 cup soured cream
100 g/3¹/2 oz sunflower seeds

1 Grease a 23 cm/9 inch square cake tin (pan) and line the base with baking parchment.

2 In a large mixing bowl, cream together the butter and caster (superfine) sugar until the mixture is light and fluffy.

3 Gradually add the beaten eggs to the mixture, beating well after each addition.

4 Sieve (strain) the self-raising flour, bicarbonate of soda (baking soda) and ground cinnamon into the creamed mixture and fold in gently, using a metal spoon.

5 Spoon in the soured cream and sunflower seeds and gently mix until well combined.

6 Spoon the mixture into the prepared cake tin (pan) and level the surface with the back of a spoon or a knife.

7 Bake in a preheated oven, 180°C/350°F/Gas Mark 4, for 45 minutes until the mixture is firm to the touch when pressed with a finger.

8 Loosen the edges with a round-bladed knife, then turn out on to a wire rack to cool completely. Slice into 12 squares.

COOK'S TIP

These moist squares will freeze well and will keep for up to 1 month.

Gingernuts

Makes 30

INGREDIENTS

350 g/12 oz/3 cups self-raising (self-rising) flour
pinch of salt
200 g/7 oz/1 cup caster (superfine) sugar

1 tbsp ground ginger
1 tsp bicarbonate of soda (baking soda)
125 g/4¹/₂ oz/¹/₂ cup butter

75 g/2³/₄ oz/¹/₄ cup golden (light corn) syrup
1 egg, beaten
1 tsp grated orange rind

1 Lightly grease several baking trays (cookie sheets).

2 Sieve (strain) the flour, salt, sugar, ginger and bicarbonate of soda (baking soda) into a large mixing bowl.

3 Heat the butter and golden (light corn) syrup together in a saucepan over a very low heat until the butter has melted.

4 Leave the butter mixture to cool

slightly, then pour it on to the dry ingredients.

5 Add the egg and orange rind and mix well.

6 Using your hands, carefully shape the dough into 30 even-sized balls.

7 Place the balls well apart on the prepared baking trays (cookie sheets), then flatten them slightly with your fingers.

8 Bake in a preheated oven, 160°C/325°F/

Gas Mark 3, for 15-20 minutes, then transfer them to a wire rack to cool.

VARIATION

If you like your gingernuts crunchy, bake them in the oven for a few minutes longer.

Caraway Biscuits (Cookies)

Makes about 36

INGREDIENTS

225 g/8 oz/2 cups plain (all-purpose) flour
pinch of salt
100 g/3½ oz/⅓ cup butter, cut into small pieces

225 g/8 oz/1¼ cups caster (superfine) sugar
1 egg, beaten

2 tbsp caraway seeds
demerara (brown crystal) sugar, for sprinkling (optional)

---

1 Lightly grease several baking trays (cookie sheets).

2 Sieve (strain) the flour and salt into a mixing bowl. Rub in the butter with your fingers until the mixture resembles fine breadcrumbs. Stir in the caster (superfine) sugar.

3 Reserve 1 tbsp beaten egg for brushing the biscuits (cookies). Add the rest of the egg and the caraway seeds to the mixture and bring together to form a soft dough.

4 On a lightly floured surface, roll out the biscuit (cookie) dough thinly and then cut out about 36 rounds with a 6 cm/2½ inch biscuit (cookie) cutter.

5 Transfer the rounds to the prepared baking trays (cookie sheets), brush with the reserved egg and sprinkle with demerara (brown crystal) sugar.

6 Bake in a preheated oven, 160°C/325°F/Gas 3, for 15 minutes until lightly golden and crisp.

7 Leave the biscuits (cookies) to cool on a wire rack and store in an airtight container.

VARIATION

Caraway seeds have a nutty, delicate anise flavour. If you don't like their flavour, replace the caraway seeds with the milder-flavoured poppy seeds.

Peanut Butter Cookies

Makes 20

INGREDIENTS

125 g/4¹/2 oz/¹/2 cup butter, softened
150 g/5¹/2 oz/¹/2 cup chunky peanut butter
225 g/8 oz/1 cup granulated sugar

1 egg, lightly beaten
150 g/5¹/2 oz/1¹/4 cup plain (all-purpose) flour
¹/2 tsp baking powder

pinch of salt
75 g/2 ³/4 oz unsalted natural peanuts, chopped

1 Lightly grease 2 baking trays (cookie sheets).

2 In a large mixing bowl, beat together the butter and peanut butter.

3 Gradually add the sugar and beat well.

4 Add the beaten egg a little at a time until it is thoroughly combined.

5 Sieve (strain) the flour, baking powder and salt into the peanut butter mixture.

6 Add the peanuts and bring all of the ingredients together to form a soft dough. Wrap and leave to chill for about 30 minutes.

7 Form the dough into 20 balls and place them on to the prepared baking trays (cookie sheets) about 5 cm/2 inches apart to allow for spreading. Flatten them slightly with your hand.

8 Bake in a preheated oven, 190°C/375°F/Gas Mark 5, for 15 minutes until golden brown. Transfer the biscuits (cookies) to a wire rack and leave to cool.

COOK'S TIP

For a crunchy bite and sparkling appearance, sprinkle the biscuits (cookies) with demerara (brown crystal) sugar before baking.

Hazelnut Squares

Makes 16

INGREDIENTS
---

150 g/5 1/2 oz/1 1/4 cups plain (all-purpose) flour
pinch of salt
1 tsp baking powder

100 g/3 1/2 oz/1/3 cup butter, cut into small pieces
150 g/5 1/2 oz/1 cup soft brown sugar
1 egg, beaten
4 tbsp milk

100 g/3 1/2 oz/1 cup hazelnuts, halved
demerara (brown crystal) sugar, for sprinkling (optional)

---

1 Grease a 23 cm/9 inch square cake tin (pan) and line the base with baking parchment.

2 Sieve (strain) the flour, salt and baking powder into a large mixing bowl.

3 Rub in the butter with your fingers until the mixture resembles fine breadcrumbs. Stir in the brown sugar.

4 Add the egg, milk and nuts to the mixture and mix well.

5 Spoon the mixture into the prepared cake tin (pan) and level the surface. Sprinkle with demerara (brown crystal) sugar, if using.

6 Bake in a preheated oven, 180°C/350°F/Gas Mark 4, for about 25 minutes or until the mixture is firm to the touch when pressed with a finger.

7 Leave to cool for 10 minutes, then loosen the edges with a round-bladed knife and turn out on to a wire rack. Cut into squares.

VARIATION

For a coffee time biscuit (cookie), replace the milk with the same amount of cold strong black coffee, the stronger the better!

Coconut Flapjacks

Makes 16 squares

INGREDIENTS

200 g/7 oz/1 cup butter
200 g /7 oz/1¹/₃ cups
    demerara (brown crystal)
    sugar

2 tbsp golden (light corn)
    syrup
275 g/9¹/₂ oz/3¹/₂ cups
    porridge oats
100 g/3¹/₂ oz/1 cup desiccated
    (shredded) coconut

75 g/2³/₄ oz/¹/₃ cup glacé
    (candied) cherries, chopped

1 Lightly grease a 30 × 23 cm/12 × 9 inch baking tray (cookie sheet).

2 Heat the butter, demerara (brown crystal) sugar and golden (light corn) syrup in a large saucepan until just melted.

3 Stir in the oats, desiccated (shredded) coconut and glacé (candied) cherries and mix until evenly combined.

4 Spread the mixture on to the baking tray (cookie sheet) and press down with the back of a palette knife (spatula) to make a smooth surface.

5 Bake in a preheated oven, 170°C/325°F/ Gas Mark 3, for about 30 minutes.

6 Remove from the oven and leave to cool on the baking tray (cookie sheet) for 10 minutes.

7 Cut the mixture into squares using a sharp knife.

8 Carefully transfer the flapjacks to a wire rack and leave to cool completely

COOK'S TIP

The flapjacks are best stored in an airtight container and eaten within 1 week. They can also be frozen for up to 1 month.

Oat & Raisin Biscuits (Cookies)

Makes 10

INGREDIENTS

50 g/1³/₄ oz/10 tsp butter
125 g/4¹/₂ oz/¹/₂ cup caster
    (superfine) sugar
1 egg, beaten

50 g/1³/₄ oz/¹/₂ cup plain (all-
    purpose) flour
¹/₂ tsp salt
¹/₂ tsp baking powder

175 g/6 oz/2 cups porridge
    oats
125 g/4¹/₂ oz/³/₄ cup raisins
2 tbsp sesame seeds

1 Lightly grease 2 baking trays (cookie sheets).

2 In a large mixing bowl, cream together the butter and sugar until light and fluffy.

3 Add the beaten egg gradually and beat until well combined.

4 Sieve (strain) the flour, salt and baking powder into the creamed mixture. Mix well.

5 Add the porridge oats, raisins and sesame seeds and mix well.

6 Place spoonfuls of the mixture well apart on the prepared baking trays (cookie sheets) and flatten them slightly with the back of a spoon.

7 Bake in a preheated oven, 180°C/350°F/Gas Mark 4, for 15 minutes.

8 Leave the biscuits (cookies) to cool slightly on the baking trays (cookie sheets).

9 Transfer the biscuits (cookies) to a wire rack and leave to cool completely before serving.

VARIATION

Substitute chopped ready-to-eat dried apricots for the raisins, if you prefer.

COOK'S TIP

To enjoy these biscuits (cookies) at their best, store them in an airtight container.

Rosemary Biscuits (Cookies)

Makes about 25

INGREDIENTS

50 g/1³/₄ oz/10 tsp butter, softened 4 tbsp caster (superfine) sugar grated rind of 1 lemon	4 tbsp lemon juice 1 egg, separated 2 tsp finely chopped fresh rosemary	200 g/7 oz/1³/₄ cups plain (all-purpose) flour, sieved (strained) caster (superfine) sugar, for sprinkling (optional)

1 Lightly grease 2 baking trays (cookie sheets).

2 In a large bowl, cream together the butter and sugar until pale and fluffy.

3 Add the lemon rind and juice, then the egg yolk and beat until they are thoroughly combined. Stir in the chopped fresh rosemary.

4 Add the sieved (strained) flour, mixing well until a soft dough is formed. Wrap and chill for 30 minutes.

5 On a lightly floured surface, roll out the dough thinly and stamp out about 25 circles with a 6 cm/2½ inch biscuit (cookie) cutter. Arrange the dough circles on the prepared baking trays (cookie sheets).

6 In a bowl, lightly whisk the egg white. Gently brush the egg white over the surface of each biscuit, then sprinkle with a little caster (superfine) sugar.

7 Bake in a preheated oven, 180°C/350°F/ Gas Mark 4, for about 15 minutes.

8 Transfer the biscuits (cookies) to a wire rack and leave to cool before serving.

VARIATION

In place of the fresh rosemary, use 1½ teaspoons of dried rosemary, if you prefer.

Citrus Crescents

Makes about 25

INGREDIENTS

100 g/3¹/₂ oz/¹/₃ cup butter, softened
75 g/2³/₄ oz/¹/₃ cup caster (superfine) sugar
1 egg, separated

200 g/7 oz/1³/₄ cups plain (all-purpose) flour
grated rind of 1 orange
grated rind of 1 lemon

grated rind of 1 lime
2-3 tbsp orange juice
caster (superfine) sugar, for sprinkling (optional)

1 Lightly grease 2 baking trays (cookie sheets).

2 In a mixing bowl, cream together the butter and sugar until light and fluffy, then gradually beat in the egg yolk.

3 Sieve (strain) the flour into the creamed mixture and mix well. Add the orange, lemon and lime rinds with enough of the orange juice to make a soft dough.

4 Roll out the dough on a lightly floured surface. Stamp out rounds using a 7.5 cm/3 inch biscuit (cookie) cutter. Make crescent shapes out of the rounds by cutting away a quarter of each round. Re-roll the trimmings to make about 25 crescents.

5 Place the crescents on to the prepared baking trays (cookie sheets). Prick the surface of each crescent with a fork.

6 Lightly whisk the egg white and brush it over the biscuits (cookies). Dust with extra caster (superfine) sugar, if using.

7 Bake in a preheated oven, 200°C/400°F/ Gas Mark 6, for about 12-15 minutes. Leave the biscuits (cookies) to cool before serving.

COOK'S TIP

Store the citrus crescents in an airtight container or freeze them for up to 1 month.

Lemon Jumbles

Makes about 50

INGREDIENTS

100 g/3¹/2 oz/¹/3 cup butter, softened
125 g/4¹/2 oz/¹/2 cup caster (superfine) sugar
grated rind of 1 lemon

1 egg, beaten
4 tbsp lemon juice
350 g/12 oz/3 cups plain (all-purpose) flour

1 tsp baking powder
1 tbsp milk
icing (confectioners') sugar, for dredging

1 Lightly grease several baking trays (cookie sheets).

2 Cream together the butter, caster sugar and lemon rind until pale and fluffy.

3 Add the beaten egg and lemon juice a little at a time, beating well after each addition.

4 Sieve (strain) the flour and baking powder into the creamed mixture and mix together. Add the milk, mixing to form a dough.

5 Turn the dough out on to a lightly floured work surface and divide into about 50 equal-sized pieces.

6 Roll each piece into a sausage shape with your hands and twist in the middle to make an 'S' shape.

7 Place on the prepared baking trays (cookie sheets) and bake in a preheated oven, 170°C/325°F/Gas Mark 3, for 15-20 minutes. Leave to cool completely on a wire rack. Dredge with icing (confectioners') sugar to serve.

VARIATION

If you prefer, shape the dough into other shapes – letters of the alphabet or geometric shapes – or just make into round biscuits (cookies).

Chocolate & Lemon Pinwheels

Makes about 40

INGREDIENTS

175 g/6 oz/³/4 cup butter,
    softened
300 g/10¹/2 oz/1¹/3 cups
    caster (superfine) sugar

1 egg, beaten
350 g/12 oz/3 cups plain (all-
    purpose) flour

25 g/1 oz dark chocolate,
    melted and cooled slightly
grated rind of 1 lemon

1 Grease and flour several baking trays (cookie sheets).

2 In a large bowl, cream together the butter and sugar until light and fluffy.

3 Gradually add the beaten egg to the creamed mixture, beating well after each addition.

4 Sieve (strain) the flour into the creamed mixture and mix until a soft dough forms.

5 Transfer half of the dough to another bowl and beat in the cooled melted chocolate.

6 Stir the grated lemon rind into the other half of the plain dough.

7 On a lightly floured surface, roll out the 2 pieces of dough to form rectangles of the same size.

8 Lay the lemon dough on top of the chocolate dough. Roll up the dough tightly into a sausage shape, using a sheet of baking parchment to guide you. Leave the dough to chill in the refrigerator.

9 Cut the roll into about 40 slices, place them on the baking trays (cookie sheets) and bake in a preheated oven, 190°C/375°F/Gas Mark 5, for 10-12 minutes or until lightly golden. Transfer the pinwheels to a wire rack and leave to cool completely before serving.

White Chocolate Cookies

Makes 24

INGREDIENTS

125 g/4^1/2 oz/^{1}/2 cup butter,
softened
125 g/4^1/2 oz/^{3}/4 cup soft
brown sugar
1 egg, beaten

200 g/7 oz/1^3/4 cups self-
raising flour
pinch of salt

125 g/4^1/2 oz white chocolate,
chopped roughly
50 g/1^3/4 oz brazil nuts,
chopped

1 Lightly grease several baking trays (cookie sheets).

2 In a large bowl, cream together the butter and sugar until light and fluffy.

3 Gradually add the beaten egg, beating well after each addition.

4 Sieve (strain) the flour and salt into the creamed mixture and blend well.

5 Stir in the chocolate and brazil nuts.

6 Place heaped teaspoons of the mixture on to the prepared baking trays (cookie sheets). Do not put more than 6 teaspoons of the mixture on to each baking tray (cookie sheet) as the cookies will spread during cooking.

7 Bake in a preheated oven, 190°C/375°F/ Gas Mark 5, for about 10-12 minutes or until just golden brown.

8 Transfer the cookies to wire racks. Leave to cool before serving.

VARIATION

*Use plain or milk chocolate
instead of white chocolate,
if you prefer.*

Shortbread Fantails

Makes 8

INGREDIENTS

125 g/4^1/$_2$ oz/^{1}/$_2$ cup butter,
  softened
40 g/1^1/$_2$ oz/8 tsp granulated
  sugar
25 g/1 oz/8 tsp icing
  (confectioners') sugar

225 g/8 oz/2 cups plain (all-
  purpose) flour
pinch of salt

2 tsp orange flower water
caster (superfine) sugar, for
  sprinkling

1 Lightly grease a
20 cm/8 inch shallow
round cake tin (pan).

2 In a large mixing bowl,
cream together the
butter, the granulated sugar
and the icing
(confectioners') sugar until
light and fluffy.

3 Sieve (strain) the flour
and salt into the
creamed mixture. Add the
orange flower water,
combine well and bring the
mixture together to form a
soft dough.

4 On a lightly floured
surface, roll out the
dough to a 20 cm/8 inch
round and place in the tin
(pan). Prick the dough well
and score into 8 triangles
with a round-bladed knife.

5 Bake in a preheated
oven, 160°C/300°F/Gas
Mark 2, for 30-35 minutes
or until the biscuit (cookie)
is pale golden and crisp.

6 Sprinkle with caster
(superfine) sugar, then
cut along the marked lines
·to make the fantails.

7 Leave the shortbread
to cool before
removing the pieces from
the tin (pan). Store in an
airtight container.

COOK'S TIP

*For a crunchy addition,
sprinkle 2 tablespoons of
chopped mixed nuts over the
top of the fantails
before baking.*

Millionaire's Shortbread

Makes 12 bars

INGREDIENTS

175 g/6 oz/1^1/$_2$ cups plain
(all-purpose) flour
125 g/4^1/$_2$ oz/^{1}/$_2$ cup butter,
cut into small pieces
50 g/1^3/$_4$ oz/3 tbsp soft brown
sugar, sieved (strained)

TOPPING:
50 g/1^3/$_4$ oz/10 tsp butter
50 g/1^3/$_4$ oz/3 tbsp soft brown
sugar

400 g/14 oz can condensed
milk
150 g/5^1/$_2$ oz milk chocolate

1 Grease a 23 cm/9 inch square cake tin (pan).

2 Sieve (strain) the flour into a mixing bowl and rub in the butter with your fingers until the mixture resembles fine breadcrumbs. Add the sugar and mix to form a firm dough.

3 Press the dough into the prepared tin (pan) and prick with a fork.

4 Bake in a preheated oven, 190°C/375°F/ Gas Mark 5, for 20 minutes until lightly golden. Leave to cool in the tin (pan).

5 To make the topping, place the butter, sugar and condensed milk in a non-stick saucepan and cook over a gentle heat, stirring constantly, until the mixture comes to the boil.

6 Reduce the heat and cook for 4-5 minutes until the caramel is pale golden and thick and is coming away from the sides of the pan. Pour the topping over the shortbread base and leave to cool.

7 When the caramel topping is firm, melt the milk chocolate in a heatproof bowl set over a saucepan of simmering water. Spread the melted chocolate over the topping, leave to set in a cool place, then cut the shortbread into squares or fingers to serve.

Vanilla Hearts

Makes about 16

INGREDIENTS

225 g/8 oz/2 cups plain (all-purpose) flour
150 g/5^1/2 oz/^{2}/3 cup butter, cut into small pieces

125 g/4^1/2 oz/^{1}/2 cup caster (superfine) sugar
1 tsp vanilla flavouring (extract)

caster (superfine) sugar, for dusting

1 Lightly grease a baking tray (cookie sheet).

2 Sieve (strain) the flour into a large mixing bowl and rub in the butter with your fingers until the mixture resembles fine breadcrumbs.

3 Stir in the caster (superfine) sugar and vanilla flavouring (extract) and bring the mixture together with your hands to make a firm dough.

4 On a lightly floured surface, roll out the dough to a thickness of 2.5 cm/1 inch. Stamp out 12 hearts with a heart-shaped biscuit cutter measuring about 5 cm/2 inches across and 2.5 cm/1 inch deep.

5 Arrange the hearts on the prepared baking tray (cookie sheet). Bake in a preheated oven, 180°C/350°F/Gas Mark 4, for 15-20 minutes until the hearts are a light golden colour.

6 Transfer the vanilla hearts to a wire rack and leave to cool. Dust with a little caster (superfine) sugar just before serving.

COOK'S TIP

Place a fresh vanilla pod in your caster (superfine) sugar and keep it in a storage jar for several weeks to give the sugar a delicious vanilla flavour.

Rock Drops

Makes 8

INGREDIENTS

200 g/7 oz/1³/4 cups plain (all-
purpose) flour
2 tsp baking powder
100 g/3¹/2 oz/¹/3 cup butter,
cut into small pieces
75 g/2³/4 oz/¹/3 cup demerara
(brown crystal) sugar

100 g/3¹/2 oz/¹/2 cup sultanas
(golden raisins)
25 g/1 oz/2 tbsp glacé
(candied) cherries, chopped
finely

1 egg, beaten
2 tbsp milk

1 Lightly grease a baking tray (cookie sheet).

2 Sieve (strain) the flour and baking powder into a mixing bowl. Rub in the butter with your fingers until the mixture resembles breadcrumbs.

3 Stir in the sugar, sultanas (golden raisins) and chopped glacé (candied) cherries.

4 Add the beaten egg and the milk to the mixture and bring together to form a soft dough.

5 Spoon 8 mounds of the mixture on to the baking tray (cookie sheet). Make sure they are spaced well apart as they will spread during cooking.

6 Bake in a preheated oven, 200°C/400°F/Gas Mark 6, for about 15-20 minutes until firm to the touch when pressed with a finger.

7 Remove the rock drops from the baking tray (cookie sheet). Either serve piping hot from the oven or transfer to a wire rack and leave to cool before serving.

COOK'S TIP

For convenience, prepare the dry ingredients in advance and just before cooking stir in the liquid.

Chocolate Chip Brownies

Makes 12

INGREDIENTS

150 g/5¹/2 oz dark chocolate, broken into pieces
225 g/8 oz/1 cup butter, softened
225 g/8 oz/2 cups self-raising flour

125 g/4¹/2 oz/¹/2 cup caster (superfine) sugar
4 eggs, beaten
75 g/2³/4 oz pistachio nuts, chopped

100 g/3¹/2 oz white chocolate, chopped roughly
icing (confectioners') sugar, for dusting

1 Lightly grease a 23 cm/9 inch baking tin (pan) and line with greaseproof paper.

2 Melt the dark chocolate and butter in a heatproof bowl set over a saucepan of simmering water. Leave to cool.

3 Sieve (strain) the flour into a separate mixing bowl and stir in the caster (superfine) sugar.

4 Stir the eggs into the melted chocolate

mixture, then pour this mixture into the flour and sugar mixture, beating well. Stir in the pistachio nuts and white chocolate, then pour the mixture into the tin (pan).

5 Bake in a preheated oven, 180°C/350°/Gas Mark 4, for 30-35 minutes until firm to the touch. Leave to cool in the tin (pan) for 20 minutes, then turn out on to a wire rack.

6 Dust the brownie with icing (confectioners')

sugar and cut into 12 pieces when cold.

COOK'S TIP

The brownie won't be completely firm in the middle when it is removed from the oven, but it will set when it has cooled.

Chocolate Biscotti

Makes 16

INGREDIENTS

1 egg
100 g/3^1/2 oz/^{1}/3 cup caster
(superfine) sugar
1 tsp vanilla flavouring
(extract)

125 g/4^1/2 oz/1 cup (all-
purpose) plain flour
^{1}/2 tsp baking powder
1 tsp ground cinnamon

50 g/1^3/4 oz dark chocolate,
chopped roughly
50 g/1^3/4 oz toasted flaked
(slivered) almonds
50 g/1^3/4 oz pine kernels
(nuts)

1 Grease a large baking tray (cookie sheet).

2 Whisk the egg, sugar and vanilla flavouring (extract) in a mixing bowl with an electric mixer until it is thick and pale – ribbons of mixture should trail from the whisk as you lift it.

3 Sieve (strain) the flour, baking powder and cinnamon into a separate bowl, then sieve (strain) into the egg mixture and fold in gently. Stir in the chocolate, almonds and pine kernels (nuts).

4 Turn out on to a lightly floured surface and shape into a flat log about 23 cm/9 inches long and 1.5 cm/^{3}/4 inch wide. Transfer to the prepared baking tray (cookie sheet).

5 Bake in a preheated oven, 180°C/350°F/ Gas Mark 4, for 20-25 minutes or until golden. Remove from the oven and leave to cool for 5 minutes or until firm.

6 Transfer the log to a cutting board. Using a serrated bread knife, cut the log on the diagonal into slices about 1 cm/ ½ inch thick and arrange them on the baking tray (cookie sheet). Cook for 10-15 minutes, turning halfway through the cooking time.

7 Leave to cool for about 5 minutes, then transfer to a wire rack to cool completely.

Chocolate Macaroons

Makes 18

INGREDIENTS

75 g/2³/4 oz dark chocolate,
broken into pieces
2 egg whites
pinch of salt

200 g/7 oz/1 cup caster
(superfine) sugar
125 g/4¹/2 oz/1¹/4 cups
ground almonds

desiccated (shredded) coconut,
for sprinkling (optional)

1 Grease 2 baking trays (cookie sheets) and line with baking parchment or rice paper.

2 Melt the dark chocolate in a small heatproof bowl set over a saucepan of simmering water. Leave to cool slightly.

3 In a mixing bowl, whisk the egg whites with the salt until they form soft peaks.

4 Gradually whisk the caster (superfine) sugar into the egg whites, then fold in the almonds and cooled melted chocolate.

5 Place heaped teaspoonfuls of the mixture spaced well apart on the prepared baking trays (cookie sheets) and spread into circles about 6 cm/2½ inches across. Sprinkle with desiccated (shredded) coconut, if using.

6 Bake in a preheated oven, 150°C/300°F/ Gas Mark 2, for about 25 minutes or until firm to the touch.

7 Leave to cool before carefully lifting from the baking trays (cookie sheets). Transfer to a wire rack and leave to cool completely before serving.

COOK'S TIP

Store the macaroons in an airtight container and eat within 1 week.

Florentines

Makes 8-10

INGREDIENTS

50 g/1³/4 oz/ 10 tsp butter
50 g/1³/4 oz/¹/4 cup caster
 (superfine) sugar
25 g/1 oz/¹/4 cup plain (all-
 purpose) flour, sieved
 (strained)

50 g/1³/4 oz/¹/3 cup almonds,
 chopped
50 g/1³/4 oz/¹/3 cup chopped
 mixed peel
25 g/1 oz/¹/4 cup raisins,
 chopped

25 g/1 oz/2 tbsp glacé
 (candied) cherries, chopped
finely grated rind of ¹/2 lemon
125 g/4¹/2 oz dark chocolate,
 melted

1 Line 2 large baking trays (cookie sheets) with baking parchment.

2 Heat the butter and caster (superfine) sugar in a small saucepan until the butter has just melted and the sugar dissolved. Remove the pan from the heat.

3 Stir in the flour and mix well. Stir in the chopped almonds, mixed peel, raisins, cherries and lemon rind. Place teaspoonfuls of the mixture well apart on the baking trays (cookie sheets).

4 Bake in a preheated oven, 180°C/350°F/Gas Mark 4, for 10 minutes or until lightly golden.

5 As soon as the florentines are removed from the oven, press the edges into neat shapes while still on the baking trays (cookie sheets), using a biscuit (cookie) cutter. Leave to cool on the baking trays (cookie sheets) until firm, then transfer to a wire rack to cool completely.

6 Spread the melted chocolate over the smooth side of each florentine. As the chocolate begins to set, mark wavy lines in it with a fork. Leave the florentines until set, chocolate side up.

Meringues

Makes about 13

INGREDIENTS

4 egg whites
pinch of salt
125 g/4^1/$_2$ oz/^{1}/$_2$ cup
    granulated sugar

125 g/4^1/$_2$ oz/^{1}/$_2$ cup caster
    (superfine) sugar

300 ml/^{1}/$_2$ pint/1^1/$_4$ cups
    double (heavy) cream,
    whipped lightly

1 Line 3 baking trays (cookie sheets) with baking parchment.

2 In a large clean bowl, whisk together the egg whites and salt until they are stiff, using an electric hand-held whisk or a balloon whisk. (You should be able to turn the bowl upside down without any movement from the egg whites.)

3 Whisk in the granulated sugar a little at a time; the meringue should start to look glossy at this stage.

4 Sprinkle in the caster (superfine) sugar a little at a time and continue whisking until all the sugar has been incorporated and the meringue is thick, white and stands in tall peaks.

5 Transfer the meringue mixture to a piping (pastry) bag fitted with a 2 cm/^{3}/$_4$ inch star nozzle (tip). Pipe about 26 small whirls on to the prepared baking trays (cookie sheets).

6 Bake in a preheated oven, 120°C/250°F/Gas Mark ^{1}/$_2$, for 1^1/$_2$ hours or until the meringues are pale golden in colour and can be easily lifted off the paper. Leave them to cool in the turned-off oven overnight.

7 Just before serving, sandwich the meringues together in pairs with the cream and arrange on a serving plate.

VARIATION

For a finer texture, replace the granulated sugar with caster (superfine) sugar.

Index

Almonds: almond cake 198
  chocolate & almond torte 178
  coffee & almond streusel cake 194
  mini frangipane tartlets with lime 60
  white chocolate & almond tart 52
apples: apple & mincemeat tart 36
  apple cake with cider 188
  apple shortcakes 202
  apple tart Tatin 32
  cheese & apple tart 30
  Eve's pudding 8
  spiced apple ring 190
apricots: apricot & cranberry
    frangipane tart 50
  apricot slices 148
  date & apricot tart 154
  white chocolate & apricot
    squares 172
asparagus & goat's cheese tart 128

Bananas: banana & date loaf 72
  orange, banana & cranberry loaf 70
biscuits (cookies) 110-52, 211-52
blackberry pudding 16
Brazil nut & mushroom pie 142
bread & butter pudding 12
breads 63-104, 146
brownies, chocolate chip 246

Cakes 152, 161-200
caraway biscuits (cookies) 218
caraway madeira 166
carrot cake 180
celery & onion pies 126
cheese: asparagus & goat's cheese
    tart 128
  cheese & apple tart 30
  cheese & chive bread 98
  cheese & ham loaf 96
  cheese & mustard scones 108
  cheese & onion pies 116
  cheese & potato bread 94
  cheese pudding 114
  cheese sables 110
  mini cheese & onion tarts 134
cheesecake, baked tofu (bean curd) 150
chilli corn bread 92
chocolate: chocolate & almond torte 178
  chocolate & lemon pinwheels 234
  chocolate & pear sponge 164
  chocolate biscotti 248
  chocolate bread 86
  chocolate brownie roulade 24
  chocolate chip brownies 246
  chocolate macaroons 250
  chocolate slab cake 176
  florentines 252
  marbled chocolate cake 192
  sticky chocolate pudding 22
  white chocolate & almond tart 52
  white chocolate & apricot
    squares 172
  white chocolate cookies 236

cinnamon & currant loaf 68
cinnamon & sunflower squares 214
cinnamon swirls 66
citrus bread 82
citrus crescents 230
clementine cake 168
coconut: coconut cake 186
  coconut cream tart 44
  coconut flapjacks 224
coffee & almond streusel cake 194
corn bread, chilli 92
cranberries: apricot & cranberry
    frangipane tart 50
  cranberry muffins 208
crème brûlée tarts 58
crown loaf 74
crumble, fruit 156
crunchy fruit cake 174
curried biscuits 112
curry pasties 140
custard tart 38

Dates: banana & date loaf 72
  date & apricot tart 154
  date & honey loaf 76

Eggless sponge 158
Eve's pudding 8

Flan, lentil & red (bell) pepper 144
flapjacks, coconut 224
florentines 252
focaccia, mini 102
frangipane tartlets 60
fruit crumble tart 28

Garlic & sage bread 146
garlic bread rolls 100
gingerbread 200
gingernuts 216
glacé (candied) fruit cake 170

Ham: cheese & ham loaf 96
  ham & cheese lattice pies 136
hazelnut squares 222

Lemon: chocolate & lemon
    pinwheels 234
  lemon jumbles 232
  lemon syrup cake 182
  lemon tart 40
lentil & red (bell) pepper flan 144

Macaroons, chocolate 250
mango twist bread 84
marbled chocolate cake 192
meringues 254
millionaire's shortbread 240
mincemeat: apple & mincemeat tart 36
  mincemeat & grape jalousie 54
mixed (candied) peel & nut tart 48
muffins, cranberry 208
mushrooms: Brazil nut & mushroom
    pie 142

Oats: coconut flapjacks 224
  oat & raisin biscuits (cookies) 226

onions: celery & onion pies 126
  cheese & onion pies 116
  mini cheese & onion tarts 134
  onion tart 130
  pissaladière 132
  red onion tart Tatin 118
orange: citrus bread 82
  citrus crescents 230
  orange, banana & cranberry loaf 70
  orange kugelhopf cake 184
  orange tart 42

Pasties, curry 140
pavlova 20
peanut butter cookies 220
pears: chocolate & pear sponge 164
  fruit crumble 156
  pear tarts 56
peppers (bell):
  lentil & red (bell) pepper flan 144
  Provençal tart 124
pies: Brazil nut & mushroom pie 142
  celery & onion pies 126
  cheese & onion pies 116
  ham & cheese lattice pies 136
  one roll fruit pie 26
  puff potato pie 120
pine kernel (nut) tart 46
pineapple upside-down cake 152
pissaladière 132
plums: fruit crumble tart 28
  plum cobbler 14
potatoes: cheese & potato bread 94
  puff potato pie 120
Provençal tart 124
puff potato pie 120
pumpkin loaf 78

Queen of puddings 10

Raspberry shortcake 18
rock drops 244
rolls: garlic bread 100
  sun-dried tomato 104
rosemary biscuits (cookies) 228

Scones 108, 202-6
shortbread 238-42
shortcake: apple 202
  raspberry 18
soda bread 88
spiced biscuits (cookies) 212
spicy bread 90
sugar-free fruit cake 196
sun-dried tomato rolls 104

Tarts 28-60, 118, 122, 124, 128, 130,
    134, 154
teacakes 64
thyme twists 106
tofu (bean curd) cheesecake 150
tomato tarts 122
treacle scones 204
treacle tart 34
tropical fruit bread 80

Vanilla hearts 242